OUR HERITAGE

A Brief History of
The Church of Jesus Christ of Latter-day Saints

D1114250

Published by
The Church of Jesus Christ of Latter-day Saints
Salt Lake City, Utah

Contents

Every prophet in this dispensation has borne witness of the divine mission of the Savior, Jesus Christ.

Introduction

The central message of this book is the message declared by The Church of Jesus Christ of Latter-day Saints since its beginning. Joseph Smith, the first prophet of this dispensation, taught:

"The fundamental principles of our religion are the testimony of the Apostles and Prophets, concerning Jesus Christ, that He died, was buried, and rose again the third day, and ascended into heaven; and all other things which pertain to our religion are only appendages to it."[1]

Every prophet who has succeeded Joseph Smith has added his personal witness of the divine mission of the Savior. The First Presidency affirmed:

"As those who are called and ordained to bear witness of Jesus Christ to all the world, we testify that He was resurrected on that Easter morning nearly two thousand years ago, and that He lives today. He has a glorified, immortal body of flesh and bones. He is the Savior, the Light and Life of the world."[2]

Millions of faithful Saints have also had testimonies of the divinity of Jesus Christ. This knowledge has motivated them to make the sacrifices necessary to build The Church of Jesus Christ of Latter-day Saints, the kingdom of God on the earth. The story of the establishment of the Church is one of faith, consecration, and joy. It is the story of living prophets who taught the truths of God to the modern world. It is the story of men and women from all walks of life who sought for the fulness of the gospel of Jesus Christ and, upon finding it, were willing to pay the price of becoming the Savior's disciples. These stalwart Saints pressed on through sufferings and hardships, witnessing even in their darkest hours of the goodness of God and the joy of his love. They have left a legacy of faith, courage, obedience, and sacrifice.

The heritage of faith continues today. Latter-day Saints throughout the world are modern pioneers in their own homelands, where they live with faith and courage in a time fraught with new challenges and opportunities. There are pages of history yet to be written. We each have an opportunity to leave a heritage for generations to follow that will help them understand the joy of living and sharing the gospel of Jesus Christ.

As we learn more about the faith of those who have gone before us, we can better understand those with whom we have joined hands in bearing witness of the Savior and helping to establish his kingdom. We can determine to live more righteously as faithful disciples of the Lord Jesus Christ.

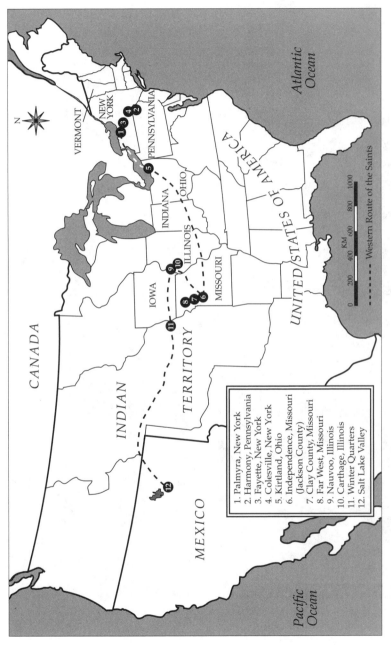

The United States of America in 1847. This map shows locations and routes of travel that were important in the early history of the Church.

1. Palmyra, New York
2. Harmony, Pennsylvania
3. Fayette, New York
4. Colesville, New York
5. Kirtland, Ohio
6. Independence, Missouri (Jackson County)
7. Clay County, Missouri
8. Far West, Missouri
9. Nauvoo, Illinois
10. Carthage, Illinois
11. Winter Quarters
12. Salt Lake Valley

------ Western Route of the Saints

Reading the scriptures led young Joseph Smith to inquire of the Lord about which church was right.

CHAPTER ONE

The First Vision

The Need for a Restoration

After the death of Jesus' Apostles, the power of the priesthood and many of the truths of the gospel were taken from the earth, beginning a long period of spiritual darkness called the great Apostasy. The prophet Amos had prophetically foreseen this loss and pronounced that the time would come when there would be "a famine in the land, not a famine of bread, nor a thirst for water, but of hearing the words of the Lord" (Amos 8:11). During the long centuries of the Apostasy, many honest men and women sought the fulness of gospel truth but were unable to find it. Clergymen of many faiths preached differing messages and called on men and women to join with them. Although most were honest in their intent, none had the fulness of the truth or the authority of God.

However, the Lord in his mercy had promised that his gospel and priesthood power would one day be restored to the earth, never to be taken away again. As the nineteenth century dawned, his promise was about to be fulfilled and the long night of apostasy was about to end.

The Courage of Young Joseph Smith

In the early 1800s, the family of Joseph and Lucy Mack Smith lived in Lebanon, New Hampshire, in the United States of America. They were humble, obscure people who earned a meager living by their hard labor. Their fifth child, Joseph Jr., was seven years old when he survived a typhoid epidemic that caused more than 3,000 deaths in the New England area. As he was recovering, a severe infection developed in the marrow of the bone in his left leg, and the almost unbearable pain lasted for more than three weeks.

The local surgeon decided that the leg would have to be amputated, but at the insistence of Joseph's mother, another doctor was sent for. Nathan Smith, a physician at nearby Dartmouth College, said that he would try to save the leg using a relatively new and extremely painful procedure to remove part of the bone. The doctor brought cords to bind the boy, but Joseph objected, saying that he would bear the operation without them. He also refused brandy, the only form of anesthetic available to him, and asked only that his father hold him in his arms during the operation.

Joseph endured the operation with great courage, and Doctor Smith, one of the most knowledgeable physicians in the country, was able to save Joseph's leg. Joseph suffered for a long time before his leg healed and he could walk without pain. After Joseph's operation, the Smith family moved to Norwich, Vermont, where they suffered three successive years of crop failure, and then moved to Palmyra, New York.

The First Vision

As a young man, Joseph Smith assisted his family in clearing land, hauling rocks, and performing a multitude of other duties. His mother, Lucy, reported that the boy Joseph was given to serious reflection and often thought about the welfare of his immortal soul. He was especially concerned about which of all the churches proselyting in the Palmyra area was right. As he explained in his own words:

"During this time of great excitement my mind was called up to serious reflection and great uneasiness; but though my feelings were deep and often poignant, still I kept myself aloof from all these parties, though I attended their several meetings as often as occasion would permit. In process of time my mind became somewhat partial to the Methodist sect, and I felt some desire to be united with them; but so great were the confusion and strife among the different denominations, that it was impossible for a person young as I was, and so unacquainted with men and things, to come to any certain conclusion who was right and who was wrong. . . .

"While I was laboring under the extreme difficulties caused by the contests of these parties of religionists, I was one day reading the Epistle of James, first chapter and fifth verse, which reads: *If any of you lack wisdom, let him ask of God, that giveth to all men liberally, and upbraideth not; and it shall be given him.*

"Never did any passage of scripture come with more power to the heart of man than this did at this time to mine. It seemed to enter with great force into every feeling of my heart. I reflected on it again and again, knowing that if any person needed wisdom from God, I did; for how to act I did not know, and unless I could get more wisdom than I then had, I would never know; for the teachers of religion of the different sects understood the same passages of scripture so differently as to destroy all confidence in settling the question by an appeal to the Bible.

"At length I came to the conclusion that I must either remain in darkness and confusion, or else I must do as James directs, that is, ask of God" (Joseph Smith—History 1:8, 11–13).

On a beautiful spring morning in 1820, alone in a grove of trees near his home, Joseph Smith knelt down and began to offer up the desires of his heart to God, asking for guidance. He described what then happened:

"Immediately I was seized upon by some power which entirely overcame me, and had such an astonishing influence over me as to bind my tongue so that I could not speak. Thick darkness gathered around me, and it seemed to me for a time as if I were doomed to sudden destruction" (JS—H 1:15).

The adversary of all righteousness knew that Joseph had a great work to do and attempted to destroy him, but Joseph, exerting all his powers, called upon God and was immediately delivered:

"At this moment of great alarm, I saw a pillar of light exactly over my head, above the brightness of the sun, which descended gradually until it fell upon me.

"It no sooner appeared than I found myself delivered from the enemy which held me bound. When the light rested upon me I saw two Personages, whose brightness and glory defy all description, standing above me in the air. One of them spake unto me, calling me by name and said, pointing to the other—*This is My Beloved Son. Hear Him!*" (JS—H 1:16–17).

As soon as Joseph gained possession of himself, he asked the Lord which of all the religious sects was right and which he should join. The Lord answered that he must join "none of them, for they were all wrong" and "all their creeds were an abomination in his sight." He said that they had a "form of godliness," but they denied "the power thereof" (JS—H 1:19). He also told Joseph many more things.

After the vision ended, Joseph found that he was lying on his back, still looking into heaven. He gradually recovered his strength and returned home.

When the sun rose on that morning in 1820, Joseph Smith could scarcely have imagined that with the coming of twilight, a prophet would once more walk the earth. He, an obscure boy living in western New York, had been chosen by God to perform the marvelous work and wonder of restoring the gospel and the Church of Jesus Christ to the earth. He had seen two divine personages and was now uniquely able to testify to the true nature of God the Father and his Son, Jesus Christ. That morning was truly the dawning of a brighter day—light had flooded a grove of trees, and God the Father and Jesus Christ had called a 14-year-old boy to be their prophet.

CHAPTER TWO

Establishing the Foundations of the Church

Coming Forth of the Book of Mormon

Visits of the Angel Moroni

On the evening of 21 September 1823, three years after receiving the First Vision, Joseph Smith prayed to the Lord for forgiveness of the follies of his youth and asked for further direction. The Lord answered by sending a heavenly messenger to instruct him. Joseph wrote:

"He called me by name, and said unto me that he was a messenger sent from the presence of God to me, and that his name was Moroni; that God had a work for me to do; and that my name should be had for good and evil among all nations, kindreds, and tongues, or that it should be both good and evil spoken of among all people.

"He said there was a book deposited, written upon gold plates, giving an account of the former inhabitants of this continent, and the source from whence they sprang. He also said that the fulness of the everlasting Gospel was contained in it, as delivered by the Savior to the ancient inhabitants" (JS—H 1:33–34).

Moroni had been the last prophet to write on this ancient record, and as directed by the Lord, he had buried it in the Hill Cumorah. He had also buried the Urim and Thummim, which was used by prophets anciently and which Joseph was to use to translate the record.

The angel directed Joseph to go to the hill, which was nearby, and told him many important things about the Lord's work in the latter days. He told Joseph that when he obtained the plates, he was not to show them to any person unless the Lord commanded

At the Hill Cumorah, Joseph Smith received the gold plates from the angel Moroni and was told to begin the work of translation.

him to do so. Moroni returned to Joseph two more times that night and once again the next day. Each time he repeated his important message and provided additional information.

On the day following the angel's visits, Joseph went to the Hill Cumorah as instructed. He said of this experience:

"On the west side of this hill, not far from the top, under a stone of considerable size, lay the plates, deposited in a stone box. This stone was thick and rounding in the middle on the upper side, and thinner towards the edges, so that the middle part of it was visible above the ground, but the edge all around was covered with earth.

"Having removed the earth, I obtained a lever, which I got fixed under the edge of the stone, and with a little exertion raised it up. I looked in, and there indeed did I behold the plates, the Urim and Thummim, and the breastplate, as stated by the messenger" (JS—H 1:51–52).

The angel Moroni appeared and told Joseph to meet him at the hill in one year at that same time and to continue the yearly meetings until the time came to receive the plates. At each visit, Moroni gave further instructions about what the Lord was going to do and how his kingdom was to be conducted (see JS—H 1:27–54).

The Work of Translation

On 22 September 1827, after four years of preparation, Moroni gave the Prophet Joseph the gold plates and told him to begin the work of translation. Emma Hale, whom Joseph had married earlier that year, accompanied him on that occasion and was waiting at the foot of the Hill Cumorah when her husband returned with the plates. She became an important help to the Prophet and acted as one of the Book of Mormon scribes for a brief period.

Because of the repeated and strenuous efforts of a local mob to steal the gold plates, Joseph and Emma were forced to leave their home in Manchester, New York. They took refuge at the home of Emma's father, Isaac Hale, in Harmony, Pennsylvania, about 120 miles southeast of Manchester. There Joseph began translating the plates. He was soon joined by his friend, Martin Harris, a well-to-do farmer, who became his scribe.

Martin asked Joseph if he could take 116 pages of translated material home to show his family members to prove to them the validity of the work they were doing. Joseph asked the Lord for permission, but the Lord's answer was no. Martin pleaded for Joseph to ask again, which Joseph reluctantly did two more times and finally received permission. Martin made a covenant to show the manuscript only to certain people, but he broke his promise, and the pages of manuscript were stolen. This loss caused Joseph inconsolable grief, for he thought that all his efforts to serve the Lord had been lost. He cried, "What shall I do? I have sinned—it is I who tempted the wrath of God. I should have been satisfied with the first answer which I received from the Lord."[1]

Joseph sincerely repented, and after a brief period when the plates and the Urim and Thummim were taken away, the Lord forgave him and he began translating once again. The Lord instructed him not to retranslate the lost material, which contained a secular history. Instead, Joseph was to translate other plates prepared by the prophet Nephi that covered the same period of time but contained greater prophecies of Christ and other sacred writings. The Lord had foreseen the loss of the 116 pages and inspired Nephi to prepare this second history. (See 1 Nephi 9; D&C 10:38–45; see also D&C 3 and 10, which were received during this period.)

At this time, Joseph was blessed with the help of Oliver Cowdery, a young schoolteacher who was directed by the Lord to the Prophet's home. Oliver commenced to write on 7 April 1829. Of that momentous time he said, "These were days never to be forgotten—to sit under the sound of a voice dictated by the inspiration of heaven, awakened the utmost gratitude of this bosom!" (JS—H 1:71, footnote).

Oliver further declared: "That book is true. . . . I wrote it myself as it fell from the lips of the Prophet. It contains the everlasting gospel, and comes in fulfillment of the revelations of John where it says he saw an angel come with the everlasting gospel to preach to every nation, tongue and people. It contains principles of salvation. And if you will walk by its light and obey its precepts you will be saved in the everlasting kingdom of God."[2]

In the midst of their work, Joseph and Oliver found that their dedication to the translation of the record had left them without food or money; they lacked even the necessary writing materials. Learning of their plight, Joseph Knight Sr., a former employer and friend of the Prophet, determined to give them assistance. He described the nature of his most timely aid:

"I bought a barrel of mackerel and some lined paper for writing. . . . I bought some nine or ten bushels of grain and five or six bushels taters [potatoes]." He then visited the two men in Harmony and recalled that "Joseph and Oliver were gone to see if they could find a place to work for provisions, but found none. They returned home and found me there with provisions, and they were glad for they were out. . . . Then they went to work and had provisions enough to last till the translation was done."[3]

Is it any wonder that the Prophet Joseph said of this righteous man: "It shall be said of him, by the sons of Zion, while there is one of them remaining, that this man was a faithful man in Israel; therefore his name shall never be forgotten."[4]

Because of increasing persecution, Joseph and Oliver left Harmony and completed the work of translation at the Peter Whitmer farm in Fayette, New York, during June 1829. The completion of this work in the midst of such trying circumstances is truly a modern-day miracle. With little formal education, Joseph Smith dictated the translation in just a little over two months of actual working time and made very few corrections. The book stands today essentially as he translated it and has been the source of testimony for millions of people throughout the world. Joseph Smith was a powerful instrument in the hands of the Lord in bringing forth the words of ancient prophets for the blessing of Saints in the latter days.

Witnesses to the Book of Mormon

While the Prophet Joseph Smith was in Fayette, the Lord revealed that Oliver Cowdery, David Whitmer, and Martin Harris were to be three special witnesses who would be permitted to see the gold plates (see 2 Nephi 27:12; Ether 5:2–4; D&C 17). They, along with Joseph, would be able to testify of the origin and truth of this ancient record.

David Whitmer explained: "We went out into the woods, near by, and sat down on a log and talked awhile. We then kneeled down and prayed. Joseph prayed. We then got up and sat on the log and were talking, when all at once a light came down from above us and encircled us for quite a little distance around; and the angel stood before us." This angel was Moroni. David said that he "was dressed in white, and spoke and called me by name and said 'Blessed is he that keepeth His commandments.' A table was set before us and on it the records were placed. The Records of the Nephites, from which the Book of Mormon was translated, the brass plates, the Ball of Directors, the sword of Laban and other plates."[5] While the men were viewing these things, they heard a voice that said: "These plates have been revealed by the power of God, and they have been translated by the power of God. The translation of them which you have seen is correct, and I command you to bear record of what you now see and hear."[6]

Soon after this event, Joseph Smith showed the plates to eight additional witnesses, who handled them in a secluded setting near the Smith family home in Manchester, New York. The testimonies of both groups of witnesses are recorded at the beginning of the Book of Mormon.

Preaching with the Book of Mormon

When the work of translation was complete, the Prophet made arrangements with Egbert B. Grandin of Palmyra to print the Book of Mormon. Martin Harris entered into a mortgage agreement with Mr. Grandin to ensure payment of the $3,000 required to print 5,000 copies of the book.

The first copies of the Book of Mormon were made available to the public at the E. B. Grandin Bookstore on 26 March 1830. Among the earliest missionaries to use the newly printed volume was Samuel Smith. In April 1830, he visited the Tomlinson Inn in the township of Mendon, New York. There he sold a copy of the book to a young man named Phinehas Young, brother of Brigham Young.

In June he retraced his steps, this time placing a copy of the Book of Mormon in the home of John P. Greene at Bloomfield, New York. John had married Rhoda Young, sister of Brigham Young. John Young, father of Brigham, next came in contact with the book, took it home, and read it through. He said that "it was the greatest work and the clearest of error of anything he had ever seen, the Bible not excepted."[7]

Although Brigham Young had been exposed to the contents of the book since the spring of 1830 by both family members and missionaries, he needed time to investigate it thoroughly. He stated: "I examined the matter studiously for two years before I made up my mind to receive that book. I knew it was true, as well as I knew that I could see with my eyes, or feel by the touch of my fingers, or be sensible of the demonstration of any sense. Had not this been the case, I never would have embraced it to this day. . . . I wished time sufficient to prove all things for myself."[8]

Brigham Young was baptized on 14 April 1832. Following his baptism and confirmation, he recalled, "According to the words of the Savior, I felt a humble, child-like spirit, witnessing unto me that my sins were forgiven."[9] He was later to become an Apostle and eventually the second President of the Church.

Restoration of the Aaronic and Melchizedek Priesthoods

When the angel Moroni first met with Joseph Smith on the Hill Cumorah in September 1823, he gave important instructions about the restoration of priesthood authority to the earth, including the following declaration: "When [the gold plates] are interpreted *the Lord will give the holy priesthood to some*, and they shall begin to proclaim this gospel and baptize by water, and after

*Peter, James, and John appeared to Joseph Smith and Oliver Cowdery
and conferred upon them the Melchizedek Priesthood.*

that they shall have power to give the Holy Ghost by the laying on of their hands."[10]

In the spring of 1829, Joseph participated in the partial fulfillment of the angel's words. As he and Oliver Cowdery were translating the Book of Mormon, they found mention of baptism for the remission of sins. On 15 May they sought further knowledge on the subject from the Lord in prayer. While offering up their petition on the banks of the Susquehanna River, the two men were visited by a heavenly messenger. He identified himself as John the Baptist of New Testament times. Laying his hands on the heads of Joseph and Oliver, he said, "Upon you my fellow servants, in the name of Messiah I confer the Priesthood of Aaron, which holds the keys of the ministering of angels, and of the gospel of repentance, and of baptism by immersion for the remission of sins" (D&C 13:1).

After this ordination, Joseph and Oliver baptized one another as commanded by John the Baptist and ordained each other to the Aaronic Priesthood. John told them that "this Aaronic Priesthood had not the power of laying on hands for the gift of the Holy Ghost, but that this should be conferred on us hereafter." He also said that "he acted under the direction of Peter, James and John, who held the keys of the Priesthood of Melchizedek, which Priesthood, he said, would in due time be conferred on us" (JS—H 1:70, 72; see also 1:68–72).

The Prophet said of this experience: "Immediately on our coming up out of the water after we had been baptized, we experienced great and glorious blessings from our Heavenly Father. No sooner had I baptized Oliver Cowdery, than the Holy Ghost fell upon him, and he stood up and prophesied many things which should shortly come to pass. And again, so soon as I had been baptized by him, I also had the spirit of prophecy, when, standing up, I prophesied concerning the rise of this Church, and many other things connected with the Church, and this generation of the children of men. We were filled with the Holy Ghost, and rejoiced in the God of our salvation" (JS—H 1:73).

Later, Peter, James, and John appeared to Joseph and Oliver and conferred upon them the Melchizedek Priesthood. They also bestowed the keys of God's kingdom upon them (see D&C 27:12–13; 128:20). The Melchizedek Priesthood is the highest authority given to men on earth. With this authority, the Prophet Joseph Smith was able to organize the Church of Jesus Christ in this dispensation and begin to establish the various priesthood quorums as they are known in the Church today.

Organization of the Church

The Lord revealed to Joseph Smith that 6 April 1830 was the day on which the Church of Jesus Christ in this dispensation was to be organized (see D&C 20:1). Notices were sent to believers and friends, and some 56 men and women gathered at the log home of Peter Whitmer Sr. in Fayette, New York. Six men were chosen by the Prophet to assist in the organization "agreeable to the laws of our country, by the will and commandments of God" (D&C 20:1).

The Prophet recorded: "Having opened the meeting by solemn prayer to our Heavenly Father, we proceeded, according to previous commandment, to call on our brethren to know whether they accepted us as their teachers in the things of the Kingdom of God, and whether they were satisfied that we should proceed and be organized as a Church according to said commandment which we had received. To these several propositions they consented by a unanimous vote."[11]

With the consent of those present, Joseph ordained Oliver an elder of the Church and Oliver ordained the Prophet an elder as they had been directed by the Lord. The sacrament was blessed and passed to the members present. Those who had been baptized were confirmed and given the gift of the Holy Ghost. The Prophet said that "the Holy Ghost was poured out upon us to a very great degree—some prophesied, whilst we all praised the Lord, and rejoiced exceedingly."[12] During this meeting, Joseph received a revelation in which the Lord instructed the Church to give heed to the words of the prophet as if they came from the Lord himself (see D&C 21:4–6).

The elements present at that meeting in 1830 continue in the Church today: exercise of the law of common consent, singing, praying, partaking of the sacrament, sharing of personal testimonies, bestowal of the gift of the Holy Ghost by the laying on of hands, ordinations, personal revelation, and revelation through priesthood officers.

Joseph's mother, Lucy Mack Smith, recorded a tender scene that occurred that day when Joseph Smith Sr., the Prophet's father, was baptized: "When Mr. Smith came out of the water, Joseph stood upon the shore, and taking his father by the hand, he exclaimed, with tears of joy, 'Praise to my God! that I have lived to see my own father baptized into the true Church of Jesus Christ!' "[13] Joseph Knight Sr. said of that moment: "[The Prophet] was filled with the Spirit to a great degree. . . . His joy seemed to be full. I think he saw the great work he had begun and was desirous to carry it out."[14]

There was a strong bond of love between father and son. Later in a eulogy to his father, the Prophet said, "I love my father and his memory; and the memory of his noble deeds rests with ponderous weight upon my mind, and many of his kind and parental words to me are written on the tablet of my heart."[15]

The love that existed between the Prophet and his father was also manifested by Joseph Smith Sr. for his father, Asael Smith. In August 1830, Joseph Smith Sr. took copies of the Book of Mormon northeast into St. Lawrence County, New York, to give to his father and mother and brothers and sisters. Asael Smith read the book nearly through before his death in October 1830 and declared that his grandson, Joseph Smith Jr., "was the very Prophet that he had long known would come in his family."[16] Three more of the sons of Asael eventually joined the Church—Silas, John, and Asael Jr. The Prophet had the privilege of seeing all his immediate family immersed in the waters of baptism, and many of his father's family.

Sidney Rigdon, who later became a member of the First Presidency, spoke of the humble beginnings of the Church and the grand vision of the future that the organizers had even then: "I met the whole church of Christ in a little old log house about 20 feet square, near Waterloo, N.Y. and we began to talk about the kingdom of God as if we had the world at our command; we talked with great confidence, . . . although we were not many people; . . . we saw by vision, the church of God, a thousand times larger; . . . the world being entirely ignorant of the testimony of the prophets and without knowledge of what God was about to do."[17]

The events that transpired on 6 April 1830 in western New York have changed the lives of millions of people. From a handful of converts in a small log house, the gospel has spread throughout the world. Now the Church is established in many lands, often in circumstances as humble as those that surrounded the original organization at Fayette. Saints across the world rejoice and find solace in the promise of the Savior: "Where two or three are gathered together in my name, . . . behold, there will I be in the midst of them" (D&C 6:32).

"Go to the Ohio": The Gathering of Latter-day Israel

Persecution in Colesville

During the very month when the Church was organized, the Prophet Joseph Smith went on a mission to teach his friends, the Joseph Knight Sr. family, who resided in Colesville, New York. On 28 June, many Knight family members and friends were prepared to make the baptismal covenant.

There was strong opposition to the preaching of the gospel in Colesville, and a mob tried to stop the baptisms by breaking down the dam the brethren had built for the purpose of holding water. This was soon repaired, however. Joseph Knight Jr. described the measures that were resorted to by enemies of the faith: "When we were going from the [baptisms], we were met by many of our neighbors, pointing at us and asking if we had been washing sheep. . . . That night our wagons were turned over and wood piled on them, and some sunk in the water, rails were piled against our doors, and chains sunk in the stream and a great deal of mischief done."[18]

At this same time, those in opposition attempted to distract the Prophet by having him arrested and tried for disturbing the peace. However, Joseph Knight Sr. hired lawyers, who soon cleared him of all charges.

Whenever important advances are being made by the Church, it seems that the adversary of all righteousness mounts a concerted effort to stop the growth of the kingdom of God. But dedicated Saints of God overcome the problems and grow stronger, as did the Colesville Saints, who welded themselves into a strong and united branch.

Missionaries to the Indians

In September and October 1830, four young men were called by revelation to take the gospel and the Book of Mormon message to the Indians of the Americas, who were descendants of the Book of Mormon people. These missionaries were Oliver Cowdery, Peter Whitmer Jr., Parley P. Pratt, and Ziba Peterson (see D&C 28:8; 30:5–6; 32). They traveled hundreds of miles under very trying conditions and were able to preach to the Catteraugus Indians near Buffalo, New York, the Wyandots of Ohio, and lastly the Delaware who lived west of the state of Missouri. But they had their greatest success with the settlers in Kirtland, Ohio, and vicinity, where they converted 127 people. After the missionaries left, the number of Saints in Ohio soon reached several hundred through the proselyting of those members left behind.

The Call to Gather to Ohio

Sidney Rigdon, a former minister and newly converted member from the Kirtland area, and a nonmember friend named Edward Partridge were anxious to meet the Prophet and learn more of the teachings of the Church. In December 1830 they traveled more than 250 miles to Fayette, New York, to visit Joseph

Smith. They asked him to seek the will of the Lord in relation to themselves and the Kirtland Saints. In response, the Lord revealed that the New York Saints should "assemble together at the Ohio" (D&C 37:3). At the third and last conference of the Church in New York, held at the Whitmer farm on 2 January 1831, the Lord repeated his directive to the members:

"And that ye might escape the power of the enemy, and be gathered unto me a righteous people, without spot and blameless —Wherefore, for this cause I gave unto you the commandment that ye should go to the Ohio; and there I will give unto you my law; and there you shall be endowed with power from on high" (D&C 38:31–32). This was the first call in this dispensation for the Saints to gather together.

While a few members chose not to dispose of their properties and make the long journey from New York to Ohio, the majority of the Saints heard the voice of the Shepherd to gather Israel. Newel Knight is representative of the disciples who followed priesthood leadership and answered the call:

"Having returned home from conference, in obedience to the commandment which had been given, I, together with the Colesville Branch, began to make preparations to go to Ohio. . . . As might be expected, we were obliged to make great sacrifices of our property. The most of my time was occupied in visiting the brethren, and helping to arrange their affairs, so that we might travel together in one company."[19]

Joseph Knight Sr. is also an example of those who willingly made sacrifices in the sale of their properties in order to join the Prophet in Ohio. His simple notice in the *Broome Republican* says much about his commitment to the gospel: "The farm lately occupied by Joseph Knight, situate in the town of Colesville, near the Colesville Bridge—bounded on one side by the Susquehanna River, and containing about one hundred and forty two acres. On said Farm are two Dwelling Houses, a good Barn, and a fine Orchard. *The terms of sale will be liberal.*"[20] Some 68 members from Colesville were on their way to Ohio by mid-April 1831.

Equally obedient to the Lord's command were 80 Saints from the Fayette Branch and 50 from the Manchester Branch, who left their homes in early May 1831. Lucy Mack Smith, mother of the Prophet, was asked to take charge of the exodus of the members from Fayette. When they arrived at Buffalo, New York, they found that the harbor on Lake Erie was clogged with an ice field, and the steamboat carrying the Fayette Saints was unable to leave port. In this difficult situation, she called upon the members to exercise their faith: "Now, brethren and sisters, if you will all of you raise your desires to heaven, that the ice may be broken up, and we be set at liberty, as sure as the Lord lives, it will be done." At that very moment a noise was heard "like bursting thunder." The ice parted and a narrow passage formed through which the boat was able to move. They had barely passed through when the avenue again closed, but they were in open water and could continue their journey. Following this miraculous escape, the company was called together in a prayer meeting to offer up their thanks to God for his mercy on their behalf.[21]

By mid-May all the branches of the Church from New York had been able to travel by ship across Lake Erie to Fairport Harbor, Ohio, where they were met by fellow Saints and taken to destinations in Kirtland and Thompson townships. The great gathering of latter-day Israel had begun. The Saints were now in a position to be taught as a body by the Lord's chosen servants, to be instructed in his laws, and to build holy temples.

The Kirtland Temple

CHAPTER THREE

Building the Kingdom in Kirtland, Ohio

The Prophet's Arrival in Ohio

On a cold day in February 1831, the Prophet Joseph Smith and his wife, Emma, then six months pregnant with twins, completed the 250-mile journey from New York to Kirtland, Ohio. They arrived in a sleigh at the Gilbert and Whitney store. The following excerpt records the meeting of Newel K. Whitney with the Prophet:

"One of the men [on the sleigh], a young and stalwart personage, alighted, and springing up the steps, walked into the store and to where the junior partner was standing.

" 'Newel K. Whitney! Thou art the man!' he exclaimed, extending his hand cordially, as if to an old and familiar acquaintance.

" 'You have the advantage of me,' replied the one addressed, as he mechanically took the proffered hand . . . —'I could not call you by name, as you have me.'

" 'I am Joseph, the Prophet,' said the stranger, smiling, 'You've prayed me here; now what do you want of me?' "[1]

Some time before, Newel and his wife, Elizabeth, had uttered a fervent prayer for guidance. In answer, the Holy Spirit descended upon them and a cloud overshadowed their house. From out of the cloud a voice proclaimed, "Prepare to receive the word of the Lord, for it is coming!"[2] Shortly thereafter, the missionaries who were called to teach the Indians came to Kirtland, and now the Prophet had arrived.

Orson F. Whitney, a grandson of Newel, later related his feelings about this event: "By what power did this remarkable man, Joseph Smith, recognize one whom he had never before seen in the flesh? Why did not Newel K. Whitney recognize him? It was because Joseph Smith was a seer, a choice seer; he had actually seen Newel K. Whitney upon his knees, hundreds of miles away, praying for his coming to Kirtland. Marvelous—but true!"[3]

The Prophet's coming brought the word of the Lord to Kirtland, where many essential elements of the Church were set in place. The basic organization of Church government was revealed, missionaries were sent abroad, the first temple was built, and many important revelations were received. The Saints were severely persecuted and tested to see whether they would demonstrate faith, courage, and willingness to follow the Lord's anointed prophet.

Two Centers of Church Activity

At the same time the Saints were being called to gather to Ohio, they began to look forward to the time when they could establish Zion. In June of 1831, the Prophet Joseph Smith received a revelation directing him, Sidney Rigdon, and 28 other elders to go on a proselyting mission to Missouri and there hold the next conference of the Church (see D&C 52). Missouri was on the western frontier of what was then the United States of America, over 1,000 miles west of Kirtland. The Lord revealed to Joseph that in Jackson County, Missouri, the Saints would receive their inheritance and establish Zion.

Joseph, the other missionaries, and shortly afterward the entire group of Saints from Colesville, New York, traveled to Jackson County during the summer of 1831 and began to establish a settlement. While the Prophet and other leaders returned to Kirtland, many members of the Church settled in Missouri.

Between 1831 and 1838, the Church had two centers of population. Joseph Smith, members of the Council of the Twelve, and a large number of Saints lived in the Kirtland, Ohio, area, while many other Church members lived in Missouri, presided over by their appointed priesthood leaders. Important events were happening in both places at the same time, and officers of the Church traveled from one location to the other as necessary. The events in Kirtland during this seven-year period will be discussed first, and then the events in Missouri during the same period will be discussed.

Sacrifices of Saints in Gathering to Ohio

Many of the Saints who came to Ohio made great sacrifices. Some were disowned by their families; others lost the companionship of former friends. Brigham Young described how he sacrificed to respond to the Prophet's call to gather:

"When we arrived in Kirtland [in September 1833], if any man that ever did gather with the Saints was any poorer than I was— it was because he had nothing. . . . I had two children to take care of—that was all. I was a widower. 'Brother Brigham, had you any shoes?' No; not a shoe to my foot, except a pair of borrowed boots. I had no winter clothing, except a homemade coat that I had had three or four years. 'Any pantaloons?' No. 'What did you do? Did you go without?' No; I borrowed a pair to wear till I could get another pair. I had travelled and preached and given away every dollar of my property. I was worth a little property when I started to preach. . . . I had traveled and preached until I had nothing left to gather with; but Joseph said: 'come up;' and I went up the best I could."[4]

Many other faithful Saints came to Kirtland, where the members already there welcomed them and willingly shared their meager substance. Such stalwart people formed the foundation for the Church's amazing growth and progress.

Revelations Received in the Kirtland Area

While the Prophet Joseph was living in the Kirtland area, he received numerous revelations, 65 of which are included in the Doctrine and Covenants. The revelations taught the Lord's will in connection with welfare, sign seeking, moral conduct, dietary principles, tithing, priesthood authority, the role of a prophet, the three degrees of glory, missionary work, the Second Coming, the law of consecration, and many other subjects.

Joseph Smith Translation of the Bible

In June 1830 Joseph Smith began his divinely commissioned work of making inspired corrections to the King James (English) Version of the Bible. This work is known as the Joseph Smith Translation of the Bible. Between June of 1830 and July of 1833, the Prophet made numerous changes to this text of the Bible, including correcting biblical language, clarifying doctrines, and restoring historical and doctrinal material.

Joseph received many revelations during the course of this work, often in response to questions that arose as he pondered scriptural passages. One such revelation occurred on 16 February 1832 after Joseph and Sidney Rigdon had translated John 5:29. They meditated upon this passage, and "the Lord touched the eyes of [their] understandings and they were opened, and the glory of the Lord shone round about" (D&C 76:19). They received one of the great visions of all time, now recorded in section 76 of the Doctrine and Covenants. They saw the Father and the Son, learned about the divine destiny of God's children, and received eternal truths about who will occupy the three kingdoms of glory.

Publishing the Revelations

At a special conference held in Hiram, Ohio, in November 1831, Church members voted to publish the Book of Commandments, containing approximately 70 revelations given to the Prophet. During this conference, the Lord gave Joseph Smith the revelations that were to be the preface and appendix to the Book of Commandments. (These later became sections 1 and 133 of the Doctrine and Covenants.)

The assignment to print the book was given to William W. Phelps, who had a printing establishment in Jackson County, Missouri. (For further information about the Book of Commandments, see page 41.) The revelations in the Book of Commandments, along with other revelations, were later printed in a volume titled the Doctrine and Covenants, which was published in Kirtland in 1835. A second edition of the Book of Mormon, with minor corrections made by the Prophet Joseph, was also printed in Kirtland.

Just a few months after the Church was organized, the Lord emphasized the important place of music in the Church by commanding the Prophet's wife, Emma, to begin making a selection of sacred hymns (see D&C 25:11). The hymnal she compiled was published in Kirtland, opening the way for the Saints to receive the Lord's promised blessing: "For my soul delighteth in the song of the heart; yea, the song of the righteous is a prayer unto me, and it shall be answered with a blessing upon their heads" (D&C 25:12).

School of the Prophets

In December 1832 and January 1833, the Prophet Joseph received the revelation that became section 88 of the Doctrine and Covenants. Among other things, this revelation directed that a "school of the prophets" (D&C 88:127) be formed to instruct the brethren in gospel doctrine and principles, the affairs of the Church, and other matters.

During the winter of 1833 the School of the Prophets met frequently, and Joseph and Emma Smith both became concerned about the brethren's customary use of tobacco, especially the cloud of tobacco smoke in meetings and lack of cleanliness caused by chewing tobacco. Joseph Smith inquired of the Lord about the matter and received the revelation that is known as the Word of Wisdom. This revelation gave the Lord's commandments for the care of the body and spirit, and promised that those who obeyed them would receive the spiritual blessings of "wisdom and great treasures of knowledge, even hidden treasures" (D&C 89:19). The Word of Wisdom also contained information about health that was not known to the medical or scientific world at the time but has since been proven to be of great benefit, such as the counsel not to use tobacco or alcohol.

Law of Consecration

In 1831 the Lord began revealing aspects of the law of consecration, a spiritual and temporal system that, if followed in righteousness, would bless the lives of the impoverished Latter-day Saints. Under this law, members of the Church were asked to consecrate, or deed, all their property to the bishop of the Church. He then granted an inheritance, or stewardship, back to the members. Families administered their stewardships as well as they could. If at the year's end they had a surplus, this was given to the bishop to use in caring for those in need. Edward Partridge was called by the Lord to serve as the first bishop of the Church.

The law of consecration consists of principles and practices that strengthen members spiritually and bring about relative economic equality, eliminating greed and poverty. Some Saints lived it well, to the blessing of themselves and others, but other members failed to rise above selfish desires, causing the eventual withdrawal of the law from the Church. In 1838 the Lord revealed the law of tithing (see D&C 119), which continues today as the financial law of the Church.

Strengthening of the Priesthood

Priesthood Offices Revealed

As the Church increased in membership, the Prophet continued to receive revelation about priesthood offices. As directed by the Lord, he organized the First Presidency, made up of himself as the President and Sidney Rigdon and Frederick G. Williams as Counselors. He also organized the Quorum of the Twelve Apostles and the First Quorum of the Seventy. He called and ordained bishops and their counselors, high priests, patriarchs, high councils, seventies, and elders. He organized the Church's first stakes.

Inexperienced, newly baptized members were often overwhelmed by calls to serve. For example, Newel K. Whitney was called as the Church's second bishop in December of 1831, to serve in Kirtland when Edward Partridge became bishop of the Saints in Missouri. Newel did not feel that he was able to carry out the requirements of the office, even though the Prophet told him that the Lord had called him by revelation. So the Prophet said to him, "Go and ask Father for yourself." Newel went and knelt in humble supplication and heard a voice from heaven that said, "Thy strength is in me."[5] He accepted the call and served as a bishop for 18 years.

Training of Leaders in Zion's Camp

The Church was in great need of priesthood leaders who had been tried, given experience, and proven faithful, who would remain true to the Lord and his prophet under any circumstances. An opportunity to prove obedience in difficult circumstances and to be trained personally by the Prophet Joseph Smith was provided by the march of Zion's Camp.

Zion's Camp was organized to help the Saints in Missouri who were being severely persecuted because of their religious beliefs. Many had been driven from their homes. (See further information on pages 39–45.) On 24 February 1834, the Lord revealed to Joseph Smith that he should organize a group of men to march from Kirtland to Missouri and help restore the Saints to their lands (see D&C 103). The Lord promised that his presence would go with them and that "all victory and glory" would be brought to pass through their "diligence, faithfulness, and prayers of faith" (D&C 103:36). Most of the original members of the Quorum of the Twelve Apostles and Quorum of the Seventy were prepared for their future responsibilities by this experience.

Zion's Camp was formally organized in New Portage, Ohio, on 6 May 1834. It eventually included 207 men, 11 women, and 11 children, whom the Prophet divided into companies of tens and fifties, instructing each group to elect a captain. One recruit, Joseph Holbrook, reported that the camp was organized "according to the ancient order of Israel."[6] For 45 days they marched together to Clay County, Missouri, a distance of over 1,000 miles. They traveled as quickly as possible and under harsh conditions. It was very difficult to get enough food. The men were often required to eat limited portions of coarse bread, rancid butter, cornmeal mush, strong honey, raw pork, rotten ham, and maggot-infested bacon and cheese. George A. Smith, who was later to become an Apostle, wrote that he was frequently hungry: "I was so weary, hungry and sleepy that I dreamed while walking along the road of seeing a beautiful stream of water by a pleasant shade tree and a nice loaf of bread and a bottle of milk laid out on a cloth by the side of the spring."[7]

The camp placed great emphasis on spirituality and obeying the commandments. On Sundays they held meetings and partook of the sacrament. The Prophet often taught the doctrines of the kingdom. He said: "God was with us, and His angels went before us, and the faith of our little band was unwavering. We know that angels were our companions, for we saw them."[8]

However, the difficulties of the camp began to take their toll on the participants. This refining process revealed the grumblers, who did not have the spirit of obedience and often faulted Joseph for their troubles. On 17 May the Prophet exhorted those who were possessed with a rebellious spirit "to humble themselves before the Lord and become united, that they might not be scourged."[9]

By 18 June the camp had reached Clay County, Missouri. However, the governor of Missouri, Daniel Dunklin, would not keep his promise to help the army of Saints reinstate the Church members who had been forced from their homes. For some in the camp, the failure of this military objective was the final test of their faith. Disappointed and angry, some openly rebelled. As a result, the Prophet warned them that the Lord would send upon them a devastating scourge. Soon a calamitous epidemic of cholera spread through the camp. Before it ended a third of the camp was afflicted, including Joseph Smith, and thereafter 14 members of the camp died. On 2 July, Joseph again warned the camp to humble themselves before the Lord and covenant to keep his commandments and said that if they did so, the plague would be stayed from that hour. The covenant was made by uplifted hands, and the plague ended.

In early July, the camp members were honorably discharged by the Prophet. The journey had revealed who was on the Lord's side and who was worthy to serve in positions of leadership. The Prophet later explained the outcome of the march: "God did not want you to fight. He could not organize his kingdom with twelve men to open the gospel door to the nations of the earth, and with seventy men under their direction to follow in their tracks, unless he took them from a body of men who had offered their lives, and who had made as great a sacrifice as did Abraham."[10]

Wilford Woodruff, a member of the camp who later became the fourth President of the Church, said: "We gained an experience that we never could have gained in any other way. We had the privilege of beholding the face of the prophet, and we had the privilege of traveling a thousand miles with him, and seeing the workings of the spirit of God with him, and the revelations of Jesus Christ unto him and the fulfilment of those revelations."[11]

In February of 1835, five months after the discharge of the camp, the Quorum of the Twelve Apostles and the First Quorum of the Seventy were organized. Seventy-nine of the eighty-two positions filled in the two quorums were filled by men who had been proven in the march of Zion's Camp.

In Kirtland, Joseph Smith continued to train future leaders. Four future Presidents of the Church—Brigham Young, John Taylor, Wilford Woodruff, and Lorenzo Snow—were baptized during the Kirtland years and later led the Church in succession until 1901. In addition, the next three Presidents—Joseph F. Smith, Heber J. Grant, and George Albert Smith, whose administrations lasted until 1951—were direct descendants of stalwart Kirtland pioneers.

Missionary Work Goes Forward

While the Saints were living in Kirtland, many missionaries were called to preach the gospel far from home, most of them at great personal sacrifice. Missionaries were sent to a number of American states, to parts of Canada, and across the Atlantic to England. Through these missionary efforts, many people received a witness of the truth of the gospel. They became valiant members who brought great strength to the young Church.

A number of revelations recorded in Kirtland included commandments to members to preach the gospel to the world. The Lord declared, "Ye shall go forth in the power of my Spirit, preaching my gospel, two by two, in my name, lifting up your voices as with the sound of a trump, declaring my word like unto angels of God" (D&C 42:6). In the following year the Lord commanded, "It becometh every man who hath been warned to warn his neighbor" (D&C 88:81).

Missions of Early Ohio Converts

Zera Pulsipher, a convert from Ohio, is an example of those who enthusiastically shared the message of the Restoration. He joined the Church in January 1832 and recorded that shortly afterward, he "was ordained to the office of an elder and went to preaching with considerable success at home and abroad."[12] He and another missionary, Elijah Cheney, traveled to the small town of Richland, New York, where they began preaching in the local school. One of the first converts baptized by Elder Pulsipher in Richland was a young farmer named Wilford Woodruff, who would one day become one of the most successful missionaries in the history of the Church and the fourth President of the Church. Within a month's time, the two missionaries had baptized a number of people and organized a branch of the Church in Richland.

Answering the call to warn their neighbors, missionaries came from all walks of life. Many of them were married and had family responsibilities. They departed in the midst of harvests and during the dead of winter, during periods of personal prosperity and at times of economic depression. A number of the elders were almost destitute when they entered the mission field. The Prophet

These four missionaries, called to take the gospel to the Indians of the Americas under very trying conditions, are examples of the sacrifices made by faithful missionaries throughout the early history of the Church.

himself traveled over 15,000 miles, serving 14 short-term missions from 1831 to 1838 in many states and in Canada.

When George A. Smith, cousin of the Prophet, received his call to the eastern United States, he was so poor that he did not own or have the means to purchase the clothes and books he needed. Consequently, the Prophet Joseph and his brother Hyrum gave him some gray cloth, and Eliza Brown made him a coat, vest, and trousers. Brigham Young gave him a pair of shoes, his father gave him a pocket Bible, and the Prophet provided a copy of the Book of Mormon.

Elders Erastus Snow and John E. Page were also poor when they left for the mission field in the spring of 1836. Describing his status at the time of his departure for a mission in western Pennsylvania, Elder Snow wrote, "I left Kirtland on foot and alone with a small suitcase containing a few Church works and a pair of socks, with five cents in my pocket, being all my worldly wealth." Elder Page told the Prophet that he could not accept a call to preach because he was destitute of clothing. He didn't even have a coat to wear. The Prophet responded by removing his coat and giving it to Elder Page. He told Elder Page to go on his mission

and the Lord would bless him abundantly.[13] On this mission, Elder
Page was blessed to share the gospel with hundreds of people
who joined the Church.

Mission of the Quorum of the Twelve Apostles

In 1835 members of the Quorum of the Twelve Apostles were
called on a mission to the eastern United States and Canada.
This is the only time in the history of the Church when all 12
members of the Quorum undertook a mission at the same time.
When they returned, Heber C. Kimball testified that they had felt
God's power and were able to heal the sick and cast out devils.

Mission to England

In the latter part of the Kirtland period, a crisis arose within
the Church. Some members, including some leaders, apostatized
because they could not bear trials and persecutions and because
they began to find fault with the Prophet Joseph and other
Church leaders. The Lord revealed to Joseph Smith that something new must be done for the salvation of his Church. That
something was an infusion of converts into the Church from
England. On Sunday, 4 June 1837, the Prophet approached
Elder Heber C. Kimball in the Kirtland Temple and said to him,
"Brother Heber, the Spirit of the Lord has whispered to me: 'Let
my servant Heber go to England and proclaim my Gospel, and
open the door of salvation to that nation.' "[14]

While Heber C. Kimball was being set apart for his mission,
Elder Orson Hyde entered the room. When he heard what was
taking place, Orson was moved upon to repent, as he had been
one of those involved in finding fault with the Prophet. He offered
to serve as a missionary and was also set apart to go to England.

So eager was Heber C. Kimball to preach the gospel on foreign
soil that as the boat approached the landing at Liverpool, England,
he leaped from the boat to the dock before it was moored, proclaiming that he was the first to reach a land overseas with the
message of the Restoration. By 23 July the missionaries were

preaching to congregations of overflow crowds and the first baptisms were scheduled for 30 July. George D. Watt won a foot-race to the River Ribble in Preston, which determined the honor of being the first to be baptized in Britain.

Within eight months, hundreds of converts had joined the Church and many branches had been organized. Reflecting on this great harvest of souls, Heber recalled that the Prophet and his Counselors "laid their hands on me and . . . said that God would make me mighty in that nation in winning souls unto Him: angels should accompany me and bear me up, that my feet should never slip; that I should be mightily blessed and prove a source of salvation to thousands."[15]

Because many early missionaries obediently accepted mission calls despite personal sacrifice, thousands of British converts enjoyed the blessings of the restored gospel. They gathered to Zion and greatly strengthened the Church for the crucial periods that lay ahead.

The Kirtland Temple

Sacrifices of the Saints

On 27 December 1832, the Saints first learned of the Lord's command to build a temple (see D&C 88:119). Construction of the temple became the main priority of the Church in Kirtland between 1833 and 1836. This presented great challenges to the Saints, who lacked both the necessary laborers and money. According to Eliza R. Snow, "At that time, . . . the Saints were few in number, and most of them very poor; and, had it not been for the assurance that God had spoken, and had commanded that a house should be built to his name, of which he not only revealed the form, but also designated the dimensions, an attempt towards building that Temple, under the then existing circumstances, would have been, by all concerned, pronounced preposterous."[16]

With faith that God would provide the necessary help and means, the Prophet Joseph Smith and the Saints began making the necessary sacrifices. John Tanner was one whom the Lord prepared to help provide the means for building the temple. John, a recent convert from Bolton, New York, in December of 1834 "received an impression by dream or vision of the night, that he was needed and must go immediately to the Church in the West. . . .

"On his arrival in Kirtland, he learned that at the time he received the impression that he must move immediately to the Church, the Prophet Joseph and some of the brethren had met in prayer-meeting and asked the Lord to send them a brother or some brethren with means to assist them to lift the mortgage on the farm upon which the temple was being built.

"The day after his arrival in Kirtland, . . . [he was] informed that the mortgage of the before mentioned farm was about to be foreclosed. Whereupon he loaned the prophet two thousand dollars and took his note on interest, with which amount the farm was redeemed."[17]

The remarkable efforts put forth by the Kirtland Saints are examples of sacrifice and consecration of time, talents, and means. For three years they labored on the building. Besides the construction skill and effort provided by the men, the women spun and knit in order to clothe those who were working. Later they made the curtains that partitioned the rooms. Construction was made more difficult by mob threats to destroy the temple, and those who worked by day guarded the temple by night. But after the Saints' immense sacrifices of time and resources, the temple was finally completed in the spring of 1836.

Dedication of the Temple

With the completion of the temple, the Lord poured out powerful spiritual blessings upon the Saints in Kirtland, including visions and the ministering of angels. Joseph Smith called this period "a year of jubilee to us, and a time of rejoicing."[18] Daniel Tyler testified, "All felt that they had a foretaste of heaven. . . . We wondered whether the millennium had commenced."[19]

The pinnacle of this outpouring of the Spirit was the dedication of the temple. An estimated 1,000 people gathered at the temple on 27 March 1836 in a spirit of rejoicing. Dedicatory anthems were sung, including "The Spirit of God Like a Fire Is Burning," which was written for the occasion by William W. Phelps. The sacrament was administered, and sermons were delivered by Sidney Rigdon, Joseph Smith, and others.

Joseph Smith read the dedicatory prayer, now recorded as Doctrine and Covenants section 109, which was given to him by revelation. In it he pleaded with the Lord that he would bless the people as he had on the day of Pentecost: "And let thy house be filled, as with a rushing mighty wind, with thy glory" (D&C 109:37). Many recorded that this prayer was fulfilled that evening when the Prophet met in the temple with members of the priesthood quorums.

Eliza R. Snow wrote: "The ceremonies of that dedication may be rehearsed, but no mortal language can describe the heavenly manifestations of that memorable day. Angels appeared to some, while a sense of divine presence was realized by all present, and each heart was filled with 'joy inexpressible and full of glory.' "[20] After the dedicatory prayer, the entire congregation rose and, with uplifted hands, shouted hosannas.

One week later, on 3 April 1836, some of the most significant events in latter-day history occurred. In the temple on that day, the Savior himself appeared to Joseph Smith and Oliver Cowdery and said, "Behold, I have accepted this house, and my name shall be here; and I will manifest myself to my people in mercy in this house" (D&C 110:7). Other great and glorious visions followed as Moses, Elias, and Elijah appeared to restore additional keys of the priesthood. Moses bestowed the keys of the gathering of Israel, Elias committed to Joseph and Oliver the dispensation of the gospel of Abraham, and Elijah restored the keys of sealing (see D&C 110:11–16). All these additional keys were necessary for the progress of the Lord's kingdom in the final dispensation of time.

The full priesthood blessings administered in the temple were not revealed or administered during the Kirtland period. These blessings were revealed to the Church through the Prophet Joseph several years later while the Nauvoo Temple was being built.

Exodus from Kirtland

The building of the temple brought many blessings, but in 1837 and 1838, faithful Saints also faced problems caused by apostasy and persecution, which hastened the end of the Church era in Kirtland.

The United States was suffering a financial depression, and the Church felt the effects. Some members became caught up in rampant speculation and debt and did not spiritually survive a dark time of economic collapse, including the collapse of the Kirtland Safety Society. This banking institution had been established by Church members in Kirtland, and some members incorrectly blamed Joseph Smith for the problems associated with it.

Organized persecution and violent mob action came from residents of the local community and from bitter members who had been excommunicated or had apostatized from the Church.

As the violence against the Saints and their leaders escalated, it became unsafe for them to remain in Kirtland. The Prophet, whose life was in grave danger, fled Kirtland in January of 1838 for Far West, Missouri. During 1838 most of the faithful Saints were also forced to leave. They left behind a monument of faith, consecration, and sacrifice in the temple built to God. In the example of their lives, they also left a permanent heritage of faithful obedience to the Lord's anointed leaders and personal sacrifice in the work of the Lord.

CHAPTER FOUR

Establishing Zion in Missouri

The Early Years in Missouri

At the same time the Saints were striving to build the kingdom of God in Kirtland, Ohio, many members of the Church were undergoing great struggles in Jackson County, Missouri.

When called upon to do so, the Saints living in Colesville, New York, had willingly left their homes to gather to Kirtland (see page 18). When they arrived in Ohio in mid-May 1831, they found that the land set aside for them was not available. The Prophet Joseph Smith took the plight of these Saints to the Lord in prayer. He had just received the revelation directing himself, Sidney Rigdon, and 28 other elders to go on a proselyting mission to Missouri, and the Lord instructed that the Colesville Saints also journey "unto the land of Missouri" (D&C 54:8). They were the first group of Saints to settle in the land that was to become known as Zion.

Newel Knight, president of the Colesville Branch, immediately gathered his people. Emily Coburn related, "We most truly were a band of pilgrims, started out to seek a better country."[1] At Wellsville, Ohio, they boarded a steamboat and, using the Ohio, Mississippi, and Missouri Rivers, traveled to Jackson County, Missouri. The captain of the steamboat said that they "were the most peaceable and quiet emigrants they had ever carried west; 'no profanity, no bad language, no gambling and no drinking.' "[2]

Using an overland route, the Prophet and other Church leaders hurried ahead of the Colesville Saints to make advance arrangements for locating them in Jackson County. The Prophet's party reached Independence, Missouri, on 14 July 1831. After viewing the country and prayerfully seeking divine guidance, the Prophet said, "[The Lord] manifested himself unto me, and designated to me and others, the very spot upon which he designed to commence the work of the gathering, and the upbuilding of an holy city, which should be called Zion."[3]

This revelation specified that Missouri was the place intended by the Lord for the gathering of the Saints, and that "the place which is now called Independence is the center place; and a spot for the temple is lying westward, upon a lot which is not far from the courthouse" (D&C 57:3). The Saints were to buy every tract of land lying west of that city to the line separating the state of Missouri and Indian territory (see D&C 57:1–5).

Joseph Smith and Bishop Partridge acquired land for the Colesville Branch in Kaw Township, some 12 miles west of Independence. On 2 August 1831, after the arrival of the branch members, a ceremony was conducted that was filled with symbolism. Twelve men, representing the 12 tribes of Israel, carried a freshly cut oak log and placed it across a stone that had been set by Oliver Cowdery, thus laying the symbolic foundation for the establishment of Zion. From that humble beginning the Saints constructed a building that was used as both a church and a schoolhouse.[4]

On the following day, a number of the brethren gathered at an elevated point one-half mile west of the Independence court-house. The Prophet Joseph Smith set in place the cornerstone for the contemplated temple and dedicated it in the name of the Lord. The central feature of the land of Zion was to be the house of the Lord.[5]

The Prophet returned to Kirtland, and the Saints in Jackson County began to receive parcels of land from Bishop Edward Partridge. They were very poor and did not even have tents to protect them from the elements while building cabins. They were also almost entirely without farm implements until teams were sent more than 200 miles east to St. Louis to obtain them. Once the Saints were outfitted, they began to break up the ground for planting. Greatly impressed by what she witnessed, Emily Coburn related: "It was a strange sight indeed, to see four or five yoke of oxen turning up the rich soil. Fencing and other improvements went on in rapid succession. Cabins were built and prepared for families as fast as time, money and labor could accomplish the work."[6]

Despite the inconveniences of the frontier, the Colesville Saints remained cheerful and happy. Parley P. Pratt, who settled with them, said: "We enjoyed many happy seasons in our prayer and other meetings, and the Spirit of the Lord was poured out upon us, and even on the little children, insomuch that many of eight, ten or twelve years of age spake, and prayed, and prophesied in our meetings and in our family worship. There was a spirit of peace and union, and love and good will manifested in this little Church in the wilderness, the memory of which will be ever dear to my heart."[7]

The Saints were blessed by a second visit from the Prophet and Sidney Rigdon in April of 1832. These leaders had just come from a very painful experience at the John Johnson farm in Hiram, Ohio, where they had been working on the translation of the Bible. A mob of enemies of the Church had dragged Joseph Smith from his home during the night. They had choked him, stripped him, and covered his body with tar and feathers. Sidney Rigdon had been dragged by his heels along frozen, rough ground, causing severe lacerations to his head.

Now, in contrast to that physical beating, they were safe with friends. Joseph affirmed that he "received a welcome only known by brethren and sisters united as one in the same faith, and by the same baptism, and supported by the same Lord. The Colesville branch, in particular, rejoiced as the ancient Saints did with Paul. It is good to rejoice with the people of God."[8]

Persecution in Jackson County

Following the commandment of the Lord, Bishop Partridge purchased hundreds of acres of land in Jackson County for the many Saints who were emigrating from Ohio and elsewhere. The leaders initially set up the Independence, Colesville, Whitmer, Big Blue, and Prairie Branches for these members. A total of ten branches were established by the latter part of 1833.[9] There were probably more than 1,000 Saints present when the combined branches met at the Big Blue River in April 1833 to celebrate the third anniversary of the founding of the Church. Newel Knight said that this gathering was the first commemoration of its kind in Zion and the Saints had a spirit of general rejoicing. However, Newel also observed, "When the Saints rejoice, the devil is mad, and his children and servants partake of his spirit."[10]

Before April had ended, the spirit of persecution manifested itself. At an early stage, local citizens warned Church members that they were displeased with the arrival of so many Latter-day Saints, who, they feared, would soon overwhelm them at the voting polls. The Saints were primarily from the northern states and generally were against black slavery, which was then legal in the state of Missouri. The Saints' belief in the Book of Mormon as scripture, their claim that Jackson County was ultimately to be their Zion, and their assertion that they were led by a prophet were very unsettling. Too, the charge that they had contact with the Indians aroused the suspicions of the local citizens.

A circular, sometimes referred to as the secret constitution, was passed around by the opposition to obtain the signatures of those willing to eliminate the "Mormon scourge." These feelings of animosity culminated on 20 July 1833 when a mob, numbering some 400 men, met at the courthouse in Independence to coordinate their efforts. Written demands were placed before the leaders of the Church calling upon the Saints to leave Jackson County; to cease printing their newspaper, *The Evening and the Morning Star;* and to not allow any additional Church members to come into Jackson County. When the mob found that the Church's leaders would not agree to these illegal requirements, they attacked the newspaper office, which was also the home of the editor, William W. Phelps. The attackers stole the printing press and demolished the building.

Destruction of the Book of Commandments

The most important project being printed at the newspaper office was the Book of Commandments, the first compilation of revelations received by the Prophet Joseph Smith. When the mob attacked the building, they tossed the unbound pages of the book into the street. Seeing this, two young Latter-day Saints, Mary Elizabeth Rollins and her sister, Caroline, at the peril of their own lives, sought to rescue what they could. Mary Elizabeth recalled:

"[The mob] brought out some large sheets of paper, and said, 'Here are the Mormon Commandments.' My sister Caroline and myself were in a corner of a fence watching them; when they spoke of the commandments I was determined to have some of them. Sister said if I went to get any of them she would go too, but said 'they will kill us.' " While the mob was busy at one end of the house, the two girls ran and filled their arms with the precious sheets. The mob saw them and ordered the girls to stop. Mary Elizabeth reported: "We ran as fast as we could. Two of them started after us. Seeing a gap in a fence, we entered into a large cornfield, laid the papers on the ground, and hid them with our persons. The corn was from five to six feet high, and very thick; they hunted around considerable, and came very near us but did not find us."

When the ruffians had gone, the girls made their way to an old log stable. Here, as reported by Mary Elizabeth, they found that "Sister Phelps and children were carrying in brush and piling it up at one side of the barn to lay her beds on. She asked me what I had—I told her. She then took them from us. . . . They got them bound in small books and sent me one, which I prized very highly."[11]

Tarring and Feathering of Bishop Partridge

The mob next seized Bishop Edward Partridge and Charles Allen. They were taken to the public square in Independence and commanded to renounce the Book of Mormon and leave the county. Bishop Partridge said, "I told them that the Saints had suffered persecution in all ages of the world; that I had done nothing which ought to offend anyone; that if they abused me, they would abuse an innocent person; that I was willing to suffer for the sake of Christ; but, to leave the country, I was not then willing to consent to it."

With this refusal, the men were stripped of their outer clothing and their bodies were covered with tar and feathers. Bishop Partridge observed, "I bore my abuse with so much resignation and meekness, that it appeared to astound the multitude, who permitted me to retire in silence, many looking very solemn, their sympathies having been touched as I thought; and as to myself, I was so filled with the Spirit and love of God, that I had no hatred towards my persecutors or anyone else."[12]

Battle of the Big Blue

The mob came again on 23 July, and Church leaders offered themselves as ransom if they would not harm the people. But the mob threatened injury to the whole Church and forced the brethren to agree that all Latter-day Saints would leave the county. As the actions of the mob were illegal, running counter to the constitutions of the United States and the state of Missouri, Church leaders sought the aid of the governor of the state, Daniel Dunklin. He advised them of their civil rights and directed the Saints to get legal counsel. Alexander W. Doniphan and others were hired to represent Church members, an action that further infuriated the mob.

At first the Latter-day Saints attempted to avoid direct conflict; however, the beatings of members and the destruction of property eventually led to a battle near the Big Blue River. Two members of the mob were killed, and the Saints lost Andrew Barber. Philo Dibble was shot three times in the stomach. Newel Knight was called to administer to him, with miraculous results. Brother Dibble related:

"Brother Newel Knight came to see me, and sat down on the side of my bed. . . . I felt the Spirit resting upon me at the crown of my head before his hand touched me, and I knew immediately that I was going to be healed. . . . I immediately arose and discharged three quarts of blood or more, with some pieces of clothes that had been driven into my body by the bullets. I then dressed myself and went out doors. . . . From that time not a drop of blood came from me and I never afterwards felt the slightest pain or inconvenience from my wounds, except that I was somewhat weak from the loss of blood."[13]

Governor Dunklin interceded and instructed Colonel Thomas Pitcher to disarm both sides. However, Colonel Pitcher's sympathies were with the mob, and he took the weapons from the Saints and delivered them to the mob. The defenseless Saints were attacked and their homes destroyed. The men had to seek refuge in the woods or suffer severe beatings. Finally Church leaders called on the people to take their belongings and flee from Jackson County.

Refuge in Clay County

In late 1833 the majority of the Saints crossed the Missouri River north into Clay County and found temporary refuge there, as described by Parley P. Pratt:

"The shore began to be lined on both sides of the ferry with men, women and children; goods, wagons, boxes, provisions, etc., while the ferry was constantly employed; and when night again closed upon us the cottonwood bottom had much the appearance of a camp meeting. Hundreds of people were seen in every direction, some in tents and some in the open air around their fires, while the rain descended in torrents. Husbands were inquiring for their wives, wives for their husbands; parents for children, and children for parents. Some had the good fortune to escape with their families, household goods, and some provisions; while others knew not the fate of their friends, and had lost all their goods. The scene . . . would have melted the hearts of any people on the earth, except our blind oppressors, and a blind and ignorant community."[14]

The opportunity to build Zion and a temple to their God in Jackson County was thus temporarily wrested from the Saints. About 1,200 Church members now did what was necessary to survive an inhospitable winter by the river in Clay County. Some took shelter in wagon boxes, tents, or dugouts in the hillside, while others occupied abandoned cabins. Newel Knight endured the winter in an Indian wigwam.

One of the first buildings constructed by the Saints in Clay County was a small log church house in which to worship. Here they "did not forget to return thanks unto Almighty God for deliverance from the hands of their vile enemies and to seek His protecting care for the future—that He would soften the hearts of the people to whom they had fled, that they might find among them something to sustain themselves."[15]

Persecution of Zion's Camp

As described in chapter 3, the Lord commanded Joseph Smith to gather a group of men to march from Kirtland to Missouri to help the Saints who had been driven from their lands in Jackson County. When Zion's Camp reached eastern Clay County, Missouri, in late June 1834, a mob of over 300 Missourians came out to meet them—intent on their destruction. Under the direction of the Prophet Joseph, the brethren set up camp at the junction of the Little and Big Fishing Rivers.

The mob began to attack with cannon fire, but the Lord was fighting the battle of the Saints. Clouds quickly began to form overhead. The Prophet described the circumstances: "It began to rain and hail. . . . The storm was tremendous; wind and rain, hail and thunder met them in great wrath, and soon softened their direful courage and frustrated all their designs to 'kill Joe Smith and his army.'. . . They crawled under wagons, into hollow trees, filled one old shanty, etc., till the storm was over, when their ammunition was soaked." After experiencing the pelting of the storm all night, "this 'forlorn hope' took the 'back track' for Independence, to join the main body of the mob, fully satisfied . . . that when Jehovah fights they would rather be absent. . . . It seemed as if the mandate of vengeance had gone forth from the God of battles, to protect His servants from the destruction of their enemies."[16]

When it became apparent that a mob army was confronting the Saints and that Governor Dunklin would not keep his promise to help them, the Prophet prayed for instruction from the Lord. The Lord told him that conditions were not then right for the redemption of Zion. The Saints had much to do to prepare their personal lives in order to build Zion. Many of them had not yet learned to be obedient to the things the Lord required: "Zion cannot be built up unless it is by the principles of the law of the celestial kingdom; otherwise I cannot receive her unto myself. And my people must needs be chastened until they learn obedience, if it must needs be, by the things which they suffer" (D&C 105:5–6).

The Lord instructed that Zion's Camp should not pursue its military objective: "In consequence of the transgressions of my people, it is expedient in me that mine elders should wait for a little season for the redemption of Zion—That they themselves may be prepared, and that my people may be taught more perfectly" (D&C 105:9–10). The brethren in Zion's Camp were honorably released, and the Prophet returned to Kirtland.

Church Headquarters at Far West

Most of the Missouri Saints continued in Clay County until 1836, when they were reminded by the citizens of that county that they had promised to remain only until they could return to Jackson County. As this now seemed impossible, they were asked to leave as pledged. Legally the Saints did not have to comply, but rather than create a conflict, they moved once again. Through the efforts of their friend in the state legislature, Alexander W. Doniphan, two new counties, named Caldwell and Daviess, were created out of Ray County in December 1836. The Saints were allowed to establish their own community of Far West, about 60 miles north of Clay County, as the county seat of Caldwell. The primary officers of the county were Latter-day Saints, and many people hoped this would end the persecutions of the Saints.

After a difficult journey from Kirtland, Ohio, the Prophet Joseph Smith arrived in Far West, Missouri, in March 1838 and established the Church headquarters there. In May he went north into Daviess County and, while visiting the Grand River, prophetically identified the area as the Valley of Adam-ondi-Ahman, the "place where Adam shall come to visit his people" (D&C 116:1).[17] Adam-ondi-Ahman became the primary community of the Saints in Daviess County. The cornerstones for a temple were dedicated at Far West on 4 July 1838, and the Saints began to feel that they had at last found a respite from their enemies.

The Battle of Crooked River

Persecution soon began again, however. On 6 August 1838, a mob of 100 people at the election polls in Gallatin, Daviess County, would not let the Saints cast their ballots. This led to a brawl in which several people were injured. The growing disorder fostered by the mob in Caldwell and Daviess Counties caused Governor Lilburn W. Boggs to bring in the state militia to keep the peace.

Captain Samuel W. Bogart, one of the militia officers, was in reality closely allied with the mob. He decided to begin a conflict by kidnapping three Latter-day Saints and holding them in his camp on the Crooked River in northwestern Ray County. A company of Latter-day Saint militia was dispatched to rescue these men, and a fierce battle was waged on 25 October 1838. Captain David W. Patten, one of the Twelve Apostles, led the company and was among those mortally wounded in the fray. David's wife, Phoebe Ann Patten; Joseph and Hyrum Smith; and Heber C. Kimball came from Far West to be with him before he died.

Heber said of David Patten: "The principles of the Gospel which were so precious to him before, afforded him that support and consolation at the time of his departure, which deprived death of its sting and horror." The dying man spoke to those at his bedside concerning some Saints who had fallen from their steadfastness into apostasy, exclaiming, " 'O that they were in my situation! For I feel that I have kept the faith.' " Next he addressed Phoebe Ann, saying, " 'Whatever you do else, Oh do not deny the faith.' " Just before he died, he prayed, " 'Father, I ask Thee in the name of Jesus Christ, that Thou wouldst release my spirit, and receive it unto Thyself.' " And then to those around him he pleaded, " 'Brethren, you have held me by your faith, but do give me up, and let me go, I beseech you.' " Brother Kimball said, "We accordingly committed him to God, and he soon breathed his last, and slept in Jesus without a groan."[18]

Captain Samuel Bogart's company had acted more like a mob than like state militia. Nevertheless, the death of a militiaman in the Battle of Crooked River, along with other reports, was employed by Governor Lilburn W. Boggs in formulating his infamous "extermination order." That decree, dated 27 October 1838, stated in part, "The Mormons must be treated as enemies, and must be exterminated or driven from the State if necessary, for the public peace—their outrages are beyond all description."[19] A militia officer was appointed to carry out the governor's order.

Haun's Mill Massacre

On 30 October 1838, three days after the extermination order was issued, some 200 men mounted a surprise attack against the small community of Saints at Haun's Mill on Shoal Creek, Caldwell County. The assailants, in an act of treachery, called for those men who wished to save themselves to run into the blacksmith shop. They then took up positions around the building and fired into it until they thought all inside were dead. Others were shot as they tried to make their escape. In all, 17 men and boys were killed and 15 wounded.

After the massacre, Amanda Smith went to the blacksmith shop, where she found her husband, Warren, and a son, Sardius, dead. Among the carnage she was overjoyed to find another son, little Alma, still alive though severely wounded. His hip had been blown away by a musket blast. With most of the men dead or wounded, Amanda knelt down and pleaded with the Lord for help:

"Oh my Heavenly Father, I cried, what shall I do? Thou seest my poor wounded boy and knowest my inexperience. Oh Heavenly Father direct me what to do!" She said that she "was directed as by a voice," instructing her to make a lye from the ashes and cleanse the wound. She then prepared a slippery elm poultice and filled the wound with it. The next day she poured the contents of a bottle of balsam into the wound.

Amanda said to her son, " 'Alma, my child, . . . you believe that the Lord made your hip?'

" 'Yes, mother.'

" 'Well, the Lord can make something there in the place of your hip, don't you believe he can, Alma?'

" 'Do you think that the Lord can, mother?' inquired the child, in his simplicity.

" 'Yes, my son,' I replied, 'he has shown it all to me in a vision.'

"Then I laid him comfortably on his face, and said: 'Now you lay like that, and don't move, and the Lord will make you another hip.'

"So Alma laid on his face for five weeks, until he was entirely recovered—a flexible gristle having grown in place of the missing joint and socket."[20]

Amanda and others had the awful task of seeing to the burial of their loved ones. Only a few able-bodied men remained, including Joseph Young, the brother of Brigham Young. Because they feared the return of the mob, there was no time to dig conventional graves. The bodies were thrown into a dry well, forming a mass grave. Joseph Young helped to carry the body of little Sardius but declared "he could not throw that boy into this horrible grave." He had played with the "interesting lad" on their journey to Missouri, and Joseph's "nature was so tender" that he could not do it. Amanda wrapped Sardius in a sheet, and the next day she and another son, Willard, placed the body in the well. Dirt and straw were then thrown in to cover the dreadful scene.[21]

At Adam-ondi-Ahman, 20-year-old Benjamin F. Johnson was spared a similar fate at the hands of a Missourian who was determined to shoot him. Benjamin had been arrested and kept under guard for eight days in intensely cold weather before an open campfire. While he was sitting on a log, a "brute" came up to him with a rifle in his hands and said, "You give up Mormonism right now, or I'll shoot you." Benjamin decisively refused, upon which the ruffian took deliberate aim at him and pulled the trigger. The gun failed to discharge. Cursing fearfully, the man declared that he had "used the gun 20 years and it had never before missed fire." Examining the lock, he reprimed the weapon and again aimed and pulled the trigger—without effect.

Following the same procedure he tried a third time, but the result was the same. A bystander told him to "fix up his gun a little" and then "you can kill the cuss all right." So for a fourth and final time the would-be murderer prepared, even putting in a fresh load. However, Benjamin declared, "This time the gun bursted and killed the wretch upon the spot." One of the Missourians was heard to say, "You'd better not try to kill that man."[22]

The Prophet Confined in Prison

Shortly after the massacre at Haun's Mill, the Prophet Joseph Smith and other leaders were taken prisoner by the state militia. A court-martial was held and the Prophet and his fellows were condemned to be shot to death by a firing squad the following morning in the town square at Far West. However, General Alexander W. Doniphan of the militia refused to carry out the shooting, calling the decision "cold-blooded murder." He warned the general who commanded the militia that if he continued his efforts to kill these men, "I will hold you responsible before an earthly tribunal, so help me God."[23]

The Prophet and the others were first taken to Independence, and then sent to Richmond, Ray County, where they were jailed awaiting trial. Parley P. Pratt was one of those with the Prophet.

While confined in Liberty Jail, the Prophet Joseph Smith pled with the Lord for the suffering Saints and received the divine direction and comfort now recorded in sections 121, 122, and 123 of the Doctrine and Covenants.

He said that one evening the guards were taunting the prisoners by telling of their deeds of rape, murder, and robbery among the Latter-day Saints. He knew that the Prophet was awake beside him and recorded that Joseph suddenly stood on his feet and rebuked the guards with great power:

" 'SILENCE, ye fiends of the infernal pit. In the name of Jesus Christ I rebuke you, and command you to be still; I will not live another minute and hear such language. Cease such talk, or you or I die THIS INSTANT!'

"He ceased to speak. He stood erect in terrible majesty. Chained, and without a weapon; calm, unruffled and dignified as an angel, he looked upon the quailing guards, whose weapons were lowered or dropped to the ground; whose knees smote together, and who, shrinking into a corner, or crouching at his feet, begged his pardon, and remained quiet till a change of guards."

Parley then observed, "I have tried to conceive of kings, of royal courts, of thrones and crowns; and of emperors assembled to decide the fate of kingdoms; but dignity and majesty have I seen but *once,* as it stood in chains, at midnight, in a dungeon in an obscure village of Missouri."[24]

When the court of inquiry was over, Joseph and Hyrum Smith, Sidney Rigdon, Lyman Wight, Caleb Baldwin, and Alexander McRae were sent to Liberty Jail in Clay County, arriving on 1 December 1838. The Prophet described their situation: "We are kept under a strong guard, night and day, in a prison of double walls and doors, proscribed in our liberty of conscience, our food is scant. . . . We have been compelled to sleep on the floor with straw, and not blankets sufficient to keep us warm. . . . The Judges have gravely told us from time to time that they knew we were innocent, and ought to be liberated, but they dare not administer the law unto us, for fear of the mob."[25]

Exodus to Illinois

While their Prophet remained imprisoned, over 8,000 Saints crossed from Missouri east into Illinois to escape the extermination order. They were forced to leave in the cold of winter, and although Brigham Young, the President of the Quorum of the Twelve, directed them and gave them every possible assistance, they suffered greatly. The John Hammer family was one of the many families who sought refuge. John recalled the difficult conditions:

"Well do I remember the sufferings and cruelties of those days. . . . Our family had one wagon, and one blind horse was all we possessed towards a team, and that one blind horse had to transport our effects to the State of Illinois. We traded our wagon with a brother who had two horses, for a light one horse wagon, this accommodating both parties. Into this small wagon we placed our clothes, bedding, some corn meal and what scanty provisions we could muster, and started out into the cold and frost to travel on foot, to eat and sleep by the wayside with the canopy of heaven for a covering. But the biting frosts of those nights and the piercing winds were less barbarous and pitiful than the demons in human form before whose fury we fled. . . . Our family, as well as many others, were almost bare-footed, and some had to wrap their feet in cloths in order to keep them from freezing and protect them from the sharp points of the frozen ground. This, at best, was very imperfect protection, and often the blood from our feet marked the frozen earth. My mother and sister were the only members of our family who had shoes, and these became worn out and almost useless before we reached the then hospitable shores of Illinois."[26]

The Prophet had to wait helplessly in prison while his people were driven from the state. The anguish of his soul is measured in his plea to the Lord, recorded in the Doctrine and Covenants, section 121:

"O God, where art thou? And where is the pavilion that covereth thy hiding place?

"How long shall thy hand be stayed, and thine eye, yea thy pure eye, behold from the eternal heavens the wrongs of thy people and of thy servants, and thine ear be penetrated with their cries?" (D&C 121:1–2).

The Lord answered him with these comforting words: "My son, peace be unto thy soul; thine adversity and thine afflictions shall be but a small moment;

"And then, if thou endure it well, God shall exalt thee on high; thou shalt triumph over all thy foes.

"Thy friends do stand by thee, and they shall hail thee again with warm hearts and friendly hands" (D&C 121:7–9).

The words of the Lord were literally fulfilled in April 1839. After six months of illegal imprisonment, changes of venue took the prisoners first to Gallatin in Daviess County, Missouri, and then toward Columbia in Boone County. However, Sheriff William Morgan was instructed "never to carry [them] to Boone County."

A person or persons in high places had determined that the prisoners would be allowed to escape, perhaps to avoid the public embarrassment of bringing them to trial when there was no evidence to convict them. The prisoners were given the opportunity to purchase two horses and elude their guards. Hyrum Smith said, "We took our change of venue for the state of Illinois, and in the course of nine or ten days arrived safe at Quincy, Adams county, where we found our families in a state of poverty, although in good health."[27] There they were indeed greeted "with warm hearts and friendly hands."

Wilford Woodruff said of his reunion with the Prophet: "Once more I had the happy privilege of taking Brother Joseph by the hand. . . . He greeted us with great joy. . . . [He] was frank, open, and familiar as usual, and our rejoicing was great. No man can understand the joyful sensations created by such a meeting, except one who has been in tribulation for the gospel's sake."[28] The Lord had miraculously preserved his Prophet and the body of the Church. Modern-day Israel began to gather once again in a new land with new opportunities and covenants before them.

The Saints built the beautiful city of Nauvoo along the banks of the Mississippi River. The Nauvoo Temple overlooked the city.

CHAPTER FIVE

Sacrifice and Blessings in Nauvoo

The Latter-day Saints who made their way to Illinois received a warm welcome from generous citizens in the town of Quincy. Following the return of the Prophet Joseph Smith from his confinement in Liberty Jail, the Saints moved north up the Mississippi River about 35 miles. There they drained the large swamps in the area and began to build the city of Nauvoo beside a bend in the river. The city was soon a bustle of activity and commerce as Saints gathered there from all parts of the United States, Canada, and England. Within four years, Nauvoo had become one of the largest cities in Illinois.

Church members lived in relative peace, secure in the fact that a prophet walked and labored among them. Hundreds of missionaries called by the Prophet left Nauvoo to proclaim the gospel. A temple was constructed, the temple endowment was received, wards were created for the first time, stakes were established, the Relief Society was organized, the book of Abraham was published, and significant revelations were received. For more than six years, the Saints displayed a remarkable degree of unity, faith, and happiness as their city became a beacon of industry and truth.

Sacrifices of Nauvoo Missionaries

As the Saints began to construct homes and plant crops, many of them became ill with the ague, an infectious disease that included fever and chills. The sick included most of the Twelve and Joseph Smith himself. On 22 July 1839 the Prophet arose from his bed of sickness with the power of God resting upon him.

Using the power of the priesthood, he healed himself and the sick in his own house, then commanded those camping in tents in his dooryard to be made whole. Many people were healed. The Prophet went from tent to tent and from house to house, blessing everyone. It was one of the great days of faith and healing in Church history.

During this period, the Prophet called the Quorum of the Twelve Apostles to go to England on missions. Elder Orson Hyde, a member of the Quorum of the Twelve, was sent to Jerusalem to dedicate Palestine for the gathering of the Jewish people and other children of Abraham. Missionaries were sent to preach throughout the United States and eastern Canada, and Addison Pratt and others received calls to go to the Pacific Islands.

These brethren made great sacrifices as they left their homes and families to respond to their calls to serve the Lord. Many members of the Twelve were struck with the ague as they prepared to depart for England. Wilford Woodruff, who was very ill, left his wife, Phoebe, almost without food and the necessities of life. George A. Smith, the youngest Apostle, was so sick that he had to be carried to the wagon, and a man who saw him asked the driver if they had been robbing the graveyard. Only Parley P. Pratt, who took his wife and children with him, his brother Orson Pratt, and John Taylor were free from disease as they left Nauvoo, although Elder Taylor later became terribly ill and almost died as they traveled to New York City.

Brigham Young was so ill that he was unable to walk even a short distance without assistance, and his companion, Heber C. Kimball, was no better. Their wives and families, too, lay suffering. When the Apostles reached the crest of a hill a short distance from their homes, both lying in a wagon, they felt as though they could not endure leaving their families in so pitiful a condition. At Heber's suggestion, they struggled to their feet, waved their hats over their heads, and shouted three times, "Hurrah, Hurrah, for Israel." Their wives, Mary Ann and Vilate, gained strength enough to stand and, leaning against the door frame, they cried out,

"Good-bye, God bless you." The two men returned to their wagon beds with a spirit of joy and satisfaction at seeing their wives standing instead of lying sick in bed.

The families remaining behind demonstrated their faith as they sacrificed to support those who had accepted mission calls. When Addison Pratt was called to a mission in the Sandwich Islands, his wife, Louisa Barnes Pratt, explained: "My four children had to be schooled and clothed, and no money would be left with me. . . . My heart felt weak at the first, but I determined to trust in the Lord, and stand bravely before the ills of life, and rejoice that my husband was counted worthy to preach the gospel."

Louisa and her children went to the dock to bid farewell to their husband and father. After they returned home, Louisa reported that "sadness took possession of our minds. It was not long till loud thunders began to roar. A family, living across the street, had a leaky house; frail and uncertain. Soon they all came over for safety through the storm. Thankful we were to see them come in; they talked comforting to us, sang hymns, and the brother prayed with us, and stayed till the storm was over."[1]

Not long after Addison's departure, his young daughter contracted smallpox. The disease was so contagious that there was real danger to any priesthood brother who might come to the Pratts, so Louisa prayed with faith and "rebuked the fever." Eleven little pimples came out on her daughter's body, but the disease never developed. In a few days the fever was gone. Louisa wrote, "I showed the child to one acquainted with that disease; he said it was an attack; that I had conquered it by faith."[2]

Those missionaries who left Nauvoo at such sacrifice brought thousands into the Church. Many of those who were converted also displayed remarkable faith and courage. Mary Ann Weston lived in England with the William Jenkins family while learning dressmaking. Brother Jenkins was converted to the gospel, and Wilford Woodruff came to the house to visit the family. Only Mary Ann was home at the time. Wilford sat by the fire and sang, "Shall I for fear of feeble man, the Spirit's course in me restrain."

Mary Ann watched him as he sang and remembered that "he looked so peaceful and happy, I thought he must be a good man, and the Gospel he preached must be true."[3]

Through her association with Church members, Mary Ann was soon converted and baptized—the only member of her family to respond to the message of the restored gospel. She married a member of the Church, who died four months later, due in part to a beating he received at the hands of a mob intent on disrupting a Church gathering. All alone, she boarded a ship filled with other Latter-day Saints bound for Nauvoo, leaving her home, her friends, and her unbelieving parents. She never saw her family again.

Her courage and commitment eventually blessed the lives of many people. She married Peter Maughan, a widower, who settled Cache Valley in northern Utah. There she raised a large, faithful family, who honored both the Church and her name.

The Standard Works

During the Nauvoo period, some of the writings that later became the Pearl of Great Price were published. This book contains selections from the book of Moses, the book of Abraham, an extract from the testimony of Matthew, excerpts from Joseph Smith's history, and the Articles of Faith. These documents were written or translated by Joseph Smith under the direction of the Lord.

The Saints now had the scriptures that would become the standard works of the Church: the Bible, the Book of Mormon, the Doctrine and Covenants, and the Pearl of Great Price. These books are of inestimable value to the children of God, for they teach the fundamental truths of the gospel and bring the honest seeker to the knowledge of God the Father and his Son, Jesus Christ. Additional revelations have been added to the modern-day scriptures as directed by the Lord through his prophets.

The Nauvoo Temple

Only 15 months after founding Nauvoo, the First Presidency, obedient to revelation, announced that the time had now come "to erect a house of prayer, a house of order, a house for the worship of our God, where the ordinances can be attended to agreeable to His divine will."[4] Though poor and struggling to provide for their own families, Latter-day Saints responded to their leaders' call and began donating time and means toward constructing a temple. More than 1,000 men donated every tenth day in labor. Louisa Decker, a young girl, was impressed that her mother sold her china dishes and a fine bed quilt as her temple contribution.[5] Other Latter-day Saints gave horses, wagons, cows, pork, and grain to aid in the temple's construction. The women of Nauvoo were asked to contribute their dimes and pennies for the temple fund.

Caroline Butler had no pennies or dimes to contribute, but she wanted very much to give something. One day while going to the city in a wagon, she saw two dead buffalo. Suddenly she knew what her temple gift could be. She and her children pulled the long hair from the buffaloes' manes and took it home with them. They washed and carded the hair and spun it into coarse yarn, then knitted eight pairs of heavy mittens that were given to the rock cutters working on the temple in the bitter winter cold.[6]

Mary Fielding Smith, wife of Hyrum Smith, wrote to Latter-day Saint women in England, who within a year gathered 50,000 pennies, weighing 434 pounds, that were shipped to Nauvoo. Farmers donated teams and wagons; others sold some of their land and donated the money to the building committee. Many watches and guns were contributed. The Saints in Norway, Illinois, sent 100 sheep to Nauvoo to be used by the temple committee.

Brigham Young remembered: "We did much hard labor on the Nauvoo temple, during which time it was difficult to get bread and other provisions for the workmen to eat." Still, President Young counseled those in charge of temple funds to give out all the flour they had, confident that the Lord would provide. Within a short time Joseph Toronto, a recent convert to the Church from Sicily, arrived in Nauvoo, bringing with him $2,500 in gold, which he laid at the feet of the Brethren.[7] These life savings of Brother Toronto were used to replenish the flour and to purchase other much needed supplies.

Shortly after the Saints arrived in Nauvoo, the Lord revealed through the Prophet Joseph Smith that baptisms could be performed for dead ancestors who had not heard the gospel (see D&C 124:29–39). Many Saints took great comfort in the promise that the dead might have the same blessings as those who accept the gospel here on earth.

The Prophet also received an important revelation concerning the teachings, covenants, and blessings that are now called the temple endowment. This sacred ordinance was to enable the Saints "to secure the fullness of those blessings" that would prepare them to "come up and abide in the presence of . . . Eloheim in the eternal worlds."[8] After receiving the endowment, husbands and wives could be sealed together by the power of the priesthood for time and all eternity. Joseph Smith realized that his time on earth was short, so while the temple was still under construction, he began giving the endowment to selected faithful followers in the upstairs room of his red brick store.

Even after the murder of the Prophet Joseph Smith, when the Saints realized they must shortly leave Nauvoo, they increased their commitment to completing the temple. The attic of the unfinished temple was dedicated as a part of the structure where the endowment would be administered. The Saints were so anxious to receive this sacred ordinance that Brigham Young, Heber C. Kimball, and others of the Twelve Apostles remained in the temple both day and night, sleeping no more than about four hours a night. Mercy Fielding Thompson had charge of the washing and ironing of temple clothes, as well as overseeing the cooking. She too lived in the temple, sometimes working throughout the night to have everything ready for the next day. Other members were just as devoted.

Why would these Saints work so hard to complete a building they would soon leave behind? Almost 6,000 Latter-day Saints received their endowments before leaving Nauvoo. As they turned their eyes toward their western migration, they were bolstered in faith and secure in the knowledge that their families were eternally sealed together. Tear-stained faces, ready to move on after burying a child or spouse on America's vast prairie, were resolute largely because of the assurances contained in the ordinances they had received in the temple.

The Relief Society

While the Nauvoo Temple was under construction, Sarah Granger Kimball, wife of Hiram Kimball, one of the city's wealthiest citizens, hired a seamstress named Margaret A. Cooke. Desiring to further the Lord's work, Sarah donated cloth to make shirts for the men working on the temple, and Margaret agreed to do the sewing. Shortly thereafter, some of Sarah's neighbors also desired to participate in the shirt making. The sisters met in the Kimball parlor and decided to formally organize. Eliza R. Snow was asked to write a constitution and bylaws for the new society.

Eliza presented the completed document to the Prophet Joseph Smith, who declared it was the best constitution he had seen. But he felt impressed to enlarge the vision of the women concerning what they could accomplish. He asked the women to attend another meeting, where he organized them into the Nauvoo Female Relief Society. Emma Smith, the Prophet's wife, became the society's first president.

Joseph told the sisters that they would receive "instruction through the order which God has established through the medium of those appointed to lead—and I now turn the key to you in the name of God and this Society shall rejoice and knowledge and intelligence shall flow down from this time—this is the beginning of better days to this Society."[9]

Soon after the society came into existence, a committee visited all of Nauvoo's poor, assessed their needs, and solicited donations to help them. Cash donations and proceeds from the sale of food and bedding provided schooling for needy children. Flax, wool, yarn, shingles, soap, candles, tinware, jewelry, baskets, quilts, blankets, onions, apples, flour, bread, crackers, and meat were donated to help those in need.

Besides helping the poor, Relief Society sisters worshiped together. Eliza R. Snow reported that in one meeting "nearly all present arose and spoke, and the spirit of the Lord like a purifying stream, refreshed every heart."[10] These sisters prayed for each other, strengthened each other's faith, and consecrated their lives and resources to help further the cause of Zion.

The Martyrdom

While the years in Nauvoo provided many happy times for the Saints, persecution soon began again, culminating in the murder of Joseph and Hyrum Smith. This was a dark and mournful time never to be forgotten. Recording her feelings upon hearing of the martyrdom, Louisa Barnes Pratt wrote: "It was a still night, and the moon was at the full. A night of death it seemed, and everything conspired to make it solemn! The voices of the officers were heard calling the men together and coming in the distance made it fall on the heart like a funeral knell. The women were assembled in groups, weeping and praying, some wishing terrible punishment on the murderers, others acknowledging the hand of God in the event."[11]

Like Louisa Barnes Pratt, many Latter-day Saints remembered the events of 27 June 1844 as a time of tears and broken hearts. The martyrdom was the most tragic event in the Church's early history. However, it was not unexpected.

On at least 19 different occasions, beginning as early as 1829, Joseph Smith told the Saints that he would probably not leave this life peacefully.[12] While he felt that his enemies would one day take his life, he did not know when. As the spring of 1844 became summer, enemies both within and without the Church worked toward Joseph's destruction. Thomas Sharp, editor of a nearby newspaper and a leader in Hancock County's anti-Mormon political party, openly called for the Prophet's murder. Citizens' groups, apostates, and civic leaders conspired to destroy the Church by destroying its prophet.

The governor of Illinois, Thomas Ford, wrote to Joseph Smith, insisting that the city council members stand trial before a non-Mormon jury on a charge of causing a civil disturbance. He said that only such a trial would satisfy the people. He promised the men complete protection, although the Prophet did not believe he could fulfill his pledge. When it appeared that there were no other alternatives, the Prophet, his brother Hyrum, John Taylor, and others submitted to arrest, fully aware that they were guilty of no crimes.

As the Prophet prepared to leave Nauvoo for the county seat of Carthage, about 20 miles away, he knew that he was seeing his family and friends for the last time. He prophesied, "I am going like a lamb to the slaughter, but I am calm as a summer's morning."[13]

As the Prophet started out, B. Rogers, who had worked on Joseph's farm for more than three years, and two other boys hiked across the fields and sat on the rail fence waiting for their friend and leader to pass by. Joseph stopped his horse beside the boys and said to the militiamen who were with him: "Gentlemen, this is my farm and these are my boys. They like me, and I like them." After shaking each boy's hand, he mounted his horse and rode on to his rendezvous with death.[14]

Dan Jones, a Welsh convert, joined the Prophet in the Carthage Jail. On 26 June 1844, the last night of his life, Joseph heard a gun fire, left the bed, and lay on the floor near Jones. The Prophet whispered, "Are you afraid to die?" "Engaged in such a cause I do not think that death would have many terrors," Jones replied. "You will yet see Wales and fulfill the mission appointed you before you die," Joseph prophesied.[15] Thousands of faithful Latter-day Saints enjoy the blessings of the Church today because Dan Jones later served an honorable and successful mission to Wales.

Shortly after five o'clock in the afternoon of 27 June 1844, a mob of about 200 men with painted faces stormed the Carthage Jail, shot and killed Joseph and his brother Hyrum, and seriously

The scene of the martyrdom at Carthage Jail. Hyrum Smith, lying in the center of the floor, was killed instantly; John Taylor, at the bottom left, was severely wounded; Joseph Smith was shot and killed as he ran toward the window; and Willard Richards, by the fireplace, remained unharmed.

wounded John Taylor. Only Willard Richards remained unharmed. Upon hearing shouts of "the Mormons are coming," the mob fled, as did most of Carthage's residents. Willard Richards cared for the wounded John Taylor, both of them mourning their slain leaders. Hyrum's body was inside the jail, while Joseph, who had fallen from a window, lay beside the outside well.

One of the first Latter-day Saints to arrive on the scene was the dead martyrs' brother Samuel. He and others helped Willard Richards prepare the bodies for the long, sorrowful journey back to Nauvoo.

Meanwhile, in Warsaw, Illinois, the James Cowley family, who were members of the Church, prepared for their evening meal. Fourteen-year-old Matthias heard about some unusual excitement in town and joined a gathering crowd. The principal speaker saw young Cowley and ordered him to go home to his mother. Boys who were not Church members followed, pelting him with rubbish before he escaped by running through a neighbor's yard.

Believing that things had quieted down, Matthias started for the river to get a pail of water. Members of the mob spotted him and paid a drunken tailor to throw him into the river. When Matthias stopped to dip the water, the tailor caught him by the back of his neck and said, "You . . . little Mormon, I'll drown you." Matthias said, "I asked him why he would drown me, and if I ever did any harm to him? No, says he, 'I won't drown you. . . . You're a good boy, you may go home.' " That night mobsters unsuccessfully attempted three times to set fire to the Cowley home, but through faith and prayers the family was protected.[16] Matthias Cowley grew and remained faithful in the Church; his son Matthias and grandson Matthew later served in the Quorum of the Twelve Apostles.

Illinois Governor Thomas Ford wrote of the martyrdom: "The murder of the Smiths, instead of putting an end to . . . the Mormons and dispersing them, as many believed it would, only bound them together closer than ever, gave them new confidence in their faith."[17] Ford also wrote, "Some gifted man like Paul, some splendid orator who will be able by his eloquence to attract crowds of the thousands, . . . may succeed in breathing a new life into [the Mormon church] and make the name of the martyred Joseph ring . . . loud and stir the souls of men." Ford lived with a fear that this would happen and that his own name would, like the names of Pilate and Herod, be "dragged down to posterity."[18] Ford's fear came true.

President John Taylor recovered from his wounds and later wrote a tribute to the slain leaders that is now section 135 of the Doctrine and Covenants. He said: "Joseph Smith, the Prophet and Seer of the Lord, has done more, save Jesus only, for the salvation of men in this world, than any other man that ever lived in it. . . . He lived great, and he died great in the eyes of God and his people; and like most of the Lord's anointed in ancient times, has sealed his mission and his works with his own blood; and so has his brother Hyrum. In life they were not divided, and in death they were not separated! . . . They lived for glory; they died for glory; and glory is their eternal reward" (D&C 135:3, 6).

Succession in the Presidency

When the Prophet Joseph and Hyrum Smith were murdered in Carthage Jail, many of the Quorum of the Twelve and other Church leaders were serving missions and were absent from Nauvoo. Several days passed before these men learned of the deaths. When Brigham Young heard the news, he knew that the keys of priesthood leadership were still with the Church, for these keys had been given to the Quorum of the Twelve. However, not all Church members understood who would replace Joseph Smith as the Lord's prophet, seer, and revelator.

Sidney Rigdon, First Counselor in the First Presidency, arrived from Pittsburgh, Pennsylvania, on 3 August 1844. In the year before this time, he had begun taking a course contrary to the counsel of the Prophet Joseph Smith and had become estranged from the Church. He refused to meet with the three members of the Twelve already in Nauvoo and instead spoke to a large group of the Saints assembled for their Sunday worship service. He told them of a vision he had received in which he had learned that no one could replace Joseph Smith. He said that a guardian to the Church should be appointed and that guardian should be Sidney Rigdon. Few Saints supported him.

Brigham Young, President of the Quorum of the Twelve Apostles, did not return to Nauvoo until 6 August 1844. He declared that he wanted only to know "what God says" about who should lead the Church.[19] The Twelve called a meeting for Thursday, 8 August 1844. Sidney Rigdon spoke in the morning session for more than one hour. He won few if any adherents to his position.

Brigham Young then spoke briefly, comforting the hearts of the Saints. As Brigham spoke, George Q. Cannon remembered, "it was the voice of Joseph himself," and "it seemed in the eyes of the people as if it were the very person of Joseph which stood before them."[20] William C. Staines testified that Brigham Young spoke like the voice of the Prophet Joseph. "I thought it was he," Staines said, "and so did thousands who heard it."[21] Wilford Woodruff also recalled that wonderful moment and wrote, "If I had not seen him with my own eyes, there is no one that could have convinced me that it was not Joseph Smith, and anyone can testify to this who was acquainted with these two men."[22] This miraculous manifestation, seen by many, made clear to the Saints that the Lord had chosen Brigham Young to succeed Joseph Smith as leader of the Church.

In the afternoon session, Brigham Young again spoke, testifying that the Prophet Joseph had ordained the Apostles to hold the keys of the kingdom of God in all the world. He prophesied that those who did not follow the Twelve would not prosper and that only the Apostles would be victorious in building up the kingdom of God.

Following his talk, President Young asked Sidney Rigdon to talk, but he chose not to. Following remarks by William W. Phelps and Parley P. Pratt, Brigham Young spoke again. He talked of completing the Nauvoo Temple, obtaining the endowment before going into the wilderness, and the importance of the scriptures. He spoke of his love for Joseph Smith and his affection for the Prophet's family. The Saints then voted unanimously in favor of the Twelve Apostles as leaders of the Church.

While a few others would claim a right to the Presidency of the Church, for most Latter-day Saints the succession crisis was over. Brigham Young, the senior Apostle and President of the Quorum of the Twelve, was the man God had chosen to lead his people, and the people had united to sustain him.

The Saints were forced by mob violence to leave their beloved city of Nauvoo.

CHAPTER SIX

Faith in Every Footstep

Preparing to Leave Nauvoo

Leaders of the Church had talked since at least 1834 about moving the Saints west to the Rocky Mountains, where they could live in peace. As the years went by, leaders discussed actual sites with explorers and studied maps to find the right place to settle. By the end of 1845, Church leaders possessed the most up-to-date information available about the West.

As persecutions in Nauvoo intensified, it became apparent that the Saints would have to leave. By November 1845, Nauvoo was bustling with the activities of preparation. Captains of hundreds, fifties, and tens were called to lead the Saints on their exodus. Each group of 100 established one or more wagon shops. Wheelwrights, carpenters, and cabinetmakers worked far into the night preparing timber and constructing wagons. Members were sent east to purchase iron, and blacksmiths constructed materials needed for the journey and farm equipment necessary to colonize a new Zion. Families collected food and housekeeping items and filled storage containers with dried fruits, flour, rice, and medicines. Working together for the common good, the Saints accomplished more than seemed possible in so short a time.

The Trials of a Winter Trek

The evacuation of Nauvoo was originally planned to take place in April 1846. But as a result of threats that the state militia intended to prevent the Saints from going west, the Twelve Apostles and other leading citizens hurriedly met in council on 2 February 1846. They agreed that it was imperative to start west immediately, and the exodus began on 4 February. Under the direction of Brigham Young, the first group of Saints eagerly began their journey. However, that eagerness faced a great test, for there were many miles to be covered before permanent camps gave them respite from late winter weather and an exceptionally rainy spring.

To seek safety from their persecutors, thousands of Saints first had to cross the wide Mississippi River to Iowa territory. The perils of their journey began early when an ox kicked a hole in a boat carrying a number of Saints and the boat sank. One observer saw the unfortunate passengers hanging on to feather beds, sticks of wood, "lumber or any thing they could get hold of and were tossed and sported on the water at the mercy of the cold and unrelenting waves. . . . Some climbed on the top of the wagon which did not go quite under and were more comfortable while the cows and oxen on board were seen swimming to the shore from whence they came."[1] Finally all the people were pulled onto boats and brought to the other side.

Two weeks after the first crossing, the river froze over for a time. Though the ice was slippery, it supported wagons and teams and made the crossing easier. But the cold weather caused much suffering as the Saints plodded through the snow. In the encampment at Sugar Creek on the other side of the river, a steady wind blew snow that fell to a depth of almost eight inches. Then a thaw caused the ground to become muddy. Around, above, and below, the elements combined to produce a miserable environment for the 2,000 Saints huddled in tents, wagons, and hastily erected shelters while they waited for the command to continue on.

The most difficult part of the journey was this early stage through Iowa. Hosea Stout recorded that he "prepared for the night by erecting a temporary tent out of bed clothes. At this time my wife was hardly able to sit up and my little son was sick with a very high fever and would not even notice any thing that was going on."[2] Many other Saints also suffered greatly.

All Is Well

The faith, courage, and determination of these Saints carried them through cold, hunger, and the deaths of loved ones. William Clayton was called to be in one of the first groups to leave Nauvoo and left his wife, Diantha, with her parents, only a month away from delivering her first child. Slogging through muddy roads and camping in cold tents wore his nerves thin as he worried about Diantha's well-being. Two months later, he still did not know if she had delivered safely but finally received the joyful word that a "fine fat boy" had been born. Almost as soon as he heard the news, William sat down and wrote a song that not only had special meaning to him but would become an anthem of inspiration and gratitude to Church members for generations. The song was "Come, Come, Ye Saints," and the famous lines expressed his faith and the faith of the thousands of Saints who sang in the midst of adversity: "All is well! All is well!"[3] They, like the members who have followed them, found the joy and peace that are the rewards of sacrifice and obedience in the kingdom of God.

Winter Quarters

It took the Saints 131 days to travel the 310 miles from Nauvoo to the settlements in western Iowa where they would pass the winter of 1846–47 and prepare for their trek to the Rocky Mountains. This experience taught them many things about travel that would help them more quickly cross the 1,000 miles of the great American plains, which was done the following year in about 111 days.

A number of settlements of Saints stretched along both sides of the Missouri River. The largest settlement, Winter Quarters, was on the west side, in Nebraska. It quickly became home to approximately 3,500 Church members, who lived in houses of logs and in dugouts of willows and dirt. As many as 2,500 Saints also lived in and around what was called Kanesville on the Iowa side of the Missouri River. Life in these settlements was almost as challenging as it had been on the trail. In the summer they suffered from malarial fever. When winter came and fresh food was no longer available, they suffered from cholera epidemics, scurvy, tooth-aches, night blindness, and severe diarrhea. Hundreds of people died.

Yet life went on. The women spent their days cleaning, ironing, washing, quilting, writing letters, preparing their few provisions for meals, and caring for their families, according to Mary Richards, whose husband, Samuel, was on a mission in Scotland. She cheerfully recorded the comings and goings of the Saints at Winter Quarters, including such activities as theological discussions, dances, Church meetings, parties, and frontier revivals.

The men worked together and met often to discuss travel plans and the future site for the settlement of the Saints. They regularly cooperated in rounding up the herds that foraged on the prairie at the outskirts of the camp. They worked in the fields, guarded the perimeters of the settlement, constructed and operated a flour mill, and readied wagons for travel, often suffering from exhaustion and illness. Some of their work was an unselfish labor of love as they prepared fields and planted crops to be harvested by the Saints who would follow them.

Brigham Young's son John called Winter Quarters "the Valley Forge of Mormondom." He lived near the burial grounds there and witnessed the "small mournful-looking trains that so often passed our door." He recalled "how poor and same-like" his family's diet of corn bread, salt bacon, and a little milk seemed. He said mush and bacon became so nauseating that eating was like taking medicine and he had difficulty swallowing.[4] Only the faith and dedication of the Saints carried them through this trying time.

Mormon Battalion

While the Saints were in Iowa, United States army recruiters asked Church leaders to provide a contingent of men to serve in the Mexican War, which had begun in May 1846. The men, who came to be called the Mormon Battalion, were to march across the southern part of the nation to California and would receive pay, clothing, and rations. Brigham Young encouraged men to participate as a way to raise money to gather the poor from Nauvoo and to aid individual soldiers' families. Cooperating with the government in this endeavor would also show the loyalty of Church members to their country and give them a justifiable reason to camp temporarily on public and Indian lands. Eventually, 541 men accepted their leaders' counsel and joined the battalion. They were accompanied by 33 women and 42 children.

The ordeal of going to war was compounded for battalion members by the sorrow of leaving their wives and children alone at a difficult time. William Hyde reflected:

"The thoughts of leaving my family at this critical time are indescribable. They were far from the land of their nativity, situated upon a lonely prairie with no dwelling but a wagon, the scorching sun beating upon them, with the prospect of the cold winds of December finding them in the same bleak, dreary place.

"My family consisted of a wife and two small children, who were left in company with an aged father and mother and a brother. The most of the Battalion left families. . . . When we were to meet with them again, God only knew. Nevertheless, we did not feel to murmur."[5]

The battalion marched 2,030 miles southwest to California, suffering from lack of food and water, insufficient rest and medical care, and the rapid pace of the march. They served as occupation troops in San Diego, San Luis Rey, and Los Angeles. At the end of their year's enlistment, they were discharged and allowed to rejoin their families. Their efforts and loyalty to the United States government gained the respect of those who led them.

After their discharge, many of the battalion members remained in California to work for a season. A number of them found their way north to the American River and were employed at John Sutter's sawmill when gold was discovered there in 1848, precipitating the famous California Gold Rush. But the Latter-day Saint brethren did not stay in California to capitalize on this opportunity for fortune. Their hearts were with their brothers and sisters struggling westward across the American plains to the Rocky Mountains. One of their number, James S. Brown, explained:

"I have never seen that rich spot of earth since; nor do I regret it, for there always has been a higher object before me than gold. . . . Some may think we were blind to our own interests; but after more than forty years we look back without regrets, although we did see fortunes in the land, and had many inducements to stay. People said, 'Here is gold on the bedrock, gold on the hills, gold in the rills, gold everywhere, . . . and soon you can make an independent fortune.' We could realize all that. Still duty called, our honor was at stake, we had covenanted with each other, there was a principle involved; for with us it was God and His kingdom first. We had friends and relatives in the wilderness, yea, in an untried, desert land, and who knew their condition? We did not. So it was duty before pleasure, before wealth, and with this prompting we rolled out."[6] These brethren knew clearly that the kingdom of God was of far greater worth than any material things of this world and chose their course accordingly.

The Brooklyn Saints

While most Saints moved to the Rocky Mountains by traveling overland from Nauvoo, a group of Saints from the eastern United States traveled a sea route. On 4 February 1846, 70 men, 68 women, and 100 children boarded the ship *Brooklyn* and sailed from New York harbor on a 17,000-mile journey to the coast of California. During their voyage two children were born, named Atlantic and Pacific, and 12 people died.

The six-month trip was very difficult. The passengers were closely crowded in the heat of the tropics, and they had only bad food and water. After rounding Cape Horn, they stopped on the island of Juan Fernandez to rest for five days. Caroline Augusta Perkins recalled that "the sight of and tread upon terra firma once more was such a relief from the ship life, that we gratefully realized and enjoyed it." They bathed and washed their clothing in the fresh water, gathered fruit and potatoes, caught fish and eels, and rambled about the island exploring a "Robinson Crusoe cave."[7]

On 31 July 1846, after a voyage marked by severe storms, dwindling food, and long days of sailing, they arrived at San Francisco. Some stayed and established a colony called New Hope, while others traveled east over the mountains to join with the Saints in the Great Basin.

The Gathering Continues

From all parts of America and from many nations, by many kinds of conveyances, on horseback or on foot, faithful converts left their homes and birthplaces to join with the Saints and begin the long journey to the Rocky Mountains.

In January 1847, President Brigham Young issued the inspired "Word and Will of the Lord concerning the Camp of Israel" (D&C 136:1), which became the constitution governing the pioneers' westward movement. Companies were organized and charged to care for the widows and fatherless in their midst. Relations with other people were to be free from evil, covetousness, and contention. The people were to be happy and show their gratitude in music, prayer, and dance. Through President Young, the Lord told the Saints, "Go thy way and do as I have told you, and fear not thine enemies" (D&C 136:17).

As the first pioneer company prepared to leave Winter Quarters, Parley P. Pratt returned from his mission to England and reported that John Taylor was following with a gift from the English Saints. The next day Brother Taylor arrived with tithing money sent by these members to aid the travelers, an evidence of their love and faith. He also brought scientific instruments that proved invaluable in charting the pioneers' journey and helping them learn about their surroundings. On 15 April 1847 the first company, led by Brigham Young, moved out. Over the next two decades, approximately 62,000 Saints would follow them across the prairies in wagons and handcarts to gather to Zion.

Wonderful sights as well as hardships awaited these travelers on their journey. Joseph Moenor recalled having "a hard time" in getting to the Salt Lake Valley. But he saw things he had never before seen—great herds of buffalo and big cedar trees on the hills.[8] Others remembered seeing vast expanses of sunflowers in bloom.

The Saints also had faith-promoting experiences that lightened the physical demands on their bodies. After a long day of travel and a meal cooked over open fires, men and women gathered in groups to discuss the day's activities. They talked about gospel principles, sang songs, danced, and prayed together.

Death frequently visited the Saints as they slowly made their way west. On 23 June 1850 the Crandall family numbered fifteen. By the week's end seven had died of the dreaded plague of cholera. In the next few days five more family members died. Then on 30 June Sister Crandall died in childbirth along with her newborn baby.

Although the Saints suffered much on their journey to the Salt Lake Valley, a spirit of unity, cooperation, and optimism prevailed. Bound together by their faith and commitment to the Lord, they found joy in the midst of their trials.

This Is the Right Place

On 21 July 1847, Orson Pratt and Erastus Snow of the first pioneer company preceded the emigrants into the Salt Lake Valley. They saw grass so deep that a person could wade through it, promising land for farming, and several creeks that wandered through the valley. Three days later, President Brigham Young, who was ill with mountain fever, was driven in his carriage to the mouth of a canyon that opened onto the valley. As President Young looked over the scene, he gave his prophetic benediction to their travels: "It is enough. This is the right place."

As the Saints who followed emerged from the mountains, they, too, gazed at their promised land! This valley with its salty lake gleaming in the western sun was the object of vision and prophecy, the land of which they and thousands after them dreamed. This was their land of refuge, where they would become a mighty people in the midst of the Rocky Mountains.

Several years later, a convert from England, Jean Rio Griffiths Baker, recorded her feelings as she viewed Salt Lake City for the first time. "The city . . . is laid out in squares or blocks as they call them here; each containing ten acres and divided into eight lots, each lot having one house. I stood and looked, I can hardly analyze my feelings, but I think my prevailing ones were joy and gratitude for the protecting care had over me and mine during our long and perilous journey."[9]

Handcart Pioneers

In the 1850s Church leaders decided to form handcart companies as a way to reduce expenses so that financial aid could be extended to the greatest number of emigrants. Saints who traveled this way put only 100 pounds of flour and a limited quantity of provisions and belongings into a cart and then pulled the cart across the plains. Between 1856 and 1860, ten handcart companies traveled to Utah. Eight of the companies reached the Salt Lake Valley successfully, but two of them, the Martin and Willie handcart companies, were caught in an early winter and many Saints among them perished.

Nellie Pucell, a pioneer in one of these ill-fated companies, turned ten years old on the plains. Both her parents died during the journey. As the group neared the mountains, the weather was bitter cold, the rations were depleted, and the Saints were too weak from hunger to continue on. Nellie and her sister collapsed. When they had almost given up hope, the leader of the company came to them in a wagon. He placed Nellie in the wagon and told Maggie to walk along beside it, holding on to steady herself. Maggie was fortunate because the forced movement saved her from frostbite.

When they reached Salt Lake City and Nellie's shoes and stockings, which she had worn across the plains, were removed, the skin came off with them as a result of frostbite. This brave girl's feet were painfully amputated and she walked on her knees the rest of her life. She later married and gave birth to six children, keeping up her own house and raising a fine posterity.[10] Her determination in spite of her situation and the kindness of those who cared for her exemplify the faith and willingness to sacrifice of these early Church members. Their example is a legacy of faith to all Saints who follow them.

A man who crossed the plains in the Martin handcart company lived in Utah for many years. One day he was in a group of people who began sharply criticizing the Church leaders for ever allowing the Saints to cross the plains with no more supplies or protection than a handcart company provided. The old man listened until he could stand no more; then he arose and said with great emotion:

"I was in that company and my wife was in it. . . . We suffered beyond anything you can imagine and many died of exposure and starvation, but did you ever hear a survivor of that company utter a word of criticism? . . . *[We] came through with the absolute knowledge that God lives for we became acquainted with him in our extremities.*

"I have pulled my handcart when I was so weak and weary from illness and lack of food that I could hardly put one foot ahead of the other. I have looked ahead and seen a patch of sand or a hill slope and I have said, I can go only that far and there I must give up, for I cannot pull the load through it. . . . I have gone on to that sand and when I reached it, the cart began pushing me. I have looked back many times to see who was pushing my cart, but my eyes saw no one. I knew then that the angels of God were there.

"Was I sorry that I chose to come by handcart? No. Neither then nor any minute of my life since. *The price we paid to become acquainted with God was a privilege to pay, and I am thankful that I was privileged to come in the Martin Handcart Company.*"[11]

Our hymnbook contains a song about the early Church members who courageously accepted the gospel and traveled far to live on the outposts of civilization:

Saints from the Salt Lake Valley risked their lives to rescue the members of the Martin handcart company, stranded on the plains by an early winter.

They, the builders of the nation,
Blazing trails along the way;
Stepping-stones for generations
Were their deeds of ev'ry day.
Building new and firm foundations,
Pushing on the wild frontier,
Forging onward, ever onward,
Blessed, honored Pioneer!

Their example teaches us how to live with more faith and courage in our own countries:

Service ever was their watchcry;
Love became their guiding star;
Courage, their unfailing beacon,
Radiating near and far.
Ev'ry day some burden lifted,
Ev'ry day some heart to cheer,
Ev'ry day some hope the brighter,
Blessed, honored Pioneer![12]

CHAPTER SEVEN

Establishing an Ensign to the Nations

Having successfully brought the first company of Saints across the plains to Utah, President Brigham Young now turned his attention to establishing God's kingdom in the desert. Through his vision and leadership, what was once an empty desert became a thriving civilization and a haven for the Saints. His plainspoken direction helped the Saints imagine the possibilities of their new home and led them forward in their quest to build God's kingdom.

Two days after the first company's arrival, Brigham Young and several of the Twelve climbed a round bluff on the mountainside that President Young had seen in vision before leaving Nauvoo. They looked out over the valley's vast expanse and prophesied that all nations of the world would be welcome in this place and that here the Saints would enjoy prosperity and peace. They named the hill Ensign Peak after the scripture in Isaiah that promised, "He shall set up an ensign for the nations, and shall assemble the outcasts of Israel" (Isaiah 11:12).[1]

President Young's first public act, on 28 July 1847, was to select a central site for a temple and put men to work planning its design and construction. Placing his cane on the chosen spot he said, "Here we shall build a temple to our God." This declaration must have comforted the Saints, who only a short time before had been forced to discontinue temple worship when they left Nauvoo.

In August, Church leaders and most of the first pioneer company returned to Winter Quarters to prepare their families to come to the valley the next year. Shortly after they arrived, Brigham Young and the Quorum of the Twelve felt impressed that the time had come to reorganize the First Presidency. As President of the Quorum of the Twelve, Brigham Young was sustained as the President of the Church. He chose Heber C. Kimball and Willard Richards as his Counselors, and the Saints unanimously sustained their leaders.

The First Year in the Valley

Two more companies of Saints arrived in the Salt Lake Valley before the summer of 1847 was over, and the almost 2,000 members were organized into the Salt Lake Stake. Late crops were planted but the harvest was marginal, and by spring many were suffering from lack of food. John R. Young, who was a boy at the time, wrote:

"By the time the grass began to grow the famine had waxed sore. For several months we had no bread. Beef, milk, pig-weeds, segoes [lily roots], and thistles formed our diet. I was the herd-boy, and while out watching the stock, I used to eat thistle stalks until my stomach would be as full as a cow's. At last the hunger was so sharp that father took down the old bird-pecked ox-hide from the limb; and it was converted into most delicious soup."[2] The settlers freely cooperated and shared with each other and so were able to survive this difficult time.

By June 1848, the settlers had planted between five and six thousand acres of land, and the valley began to look green and productive. But to the Saints' dismay, huge hordes of black crickets descended upon the crops. The settlers did everything they could. They dug trenches and turned streams of water on the crickets. They clubbed the insects with sticks and brooms and tried to burn them, but their efforts were useless. The crickets continued to come in seemingly endless numbers. Patriarch John Smith, president of the Salt Lake Stake, called for a day of fasting and prayer. Soon large flocks of seagulls appeared in the sky and descended on the crickets. Susan Noble Grant said of the experience: "To our astonishment, the gulls seemed almost ravenous while gobbling down the scrambling, hopping crickets."[3] The Saints watched in joy and wonderment. Their lives had been saved.

Through their faith and industry, the Saints began to establish a city in the Salt Lake Valley. This engraving shows the valley in 1853.

The Saints worked with energy and faith despite their difficult circumstances, and soon they had made great progress. A traveler on his way to California passed through Salt Lake City in September 1849 and paid tribute to them in this way: "A more orderly, earnest, industrious and civil people, I have never been among than these, and it is incredible how much they have done here in the wilderness in so short a time. In this city which contains about from four to five thousand inhabitants, I have not met in a citizen a single idler, or any person who looks like a loafer. Their prospects for crops are fair, and there is a spirit and energy in all that you see that cannot be equaled in any city of any size that I have ever been in."[4]

Explorations

In the late summer of 1848, President Brigham Young again made the journey from Winter Quarters to the Salt Lake Valley. When he arrived, he realized that the Saints needed to learn what resources were available in their new environment. Much was gained from Indians who lived in the area, but President Young also sent Church members on explorations to discover the medicinal properties of plants and the natural resources available.

He sent other exploring parties to find settlement sites. In their travels these members discovered mineral deposits, abundant timber, water sources, and grasslands, as well as suitable areas for settlement. To guard against land speculation, the prophet warned the Saints against cutting up their assigned property to sell to others. The land was their stewardship and was to be managed wisely and industriously, not for financial gain.

In the fall of 1849, the Perpetual Emigrating Fund was established under the direction of President Young. Its purpose was to assist the poor who did not have the means to travel to join the body of the Church. At great sacrifice, many Saints contributed to the fund, and as a result, thousands of members were able to travel to the Salt Lake Valley. As soon as they were able, those who received help were expected to repay the amount of assistance they had received. These funds were used to help still others. Through this cooperative effort, the Saints blessed the lives of those in need.

Missionaries Answer the Call

With the hum of labor and domestic life filling the air, President Brigham Young turned to the concerns of the Church. At the general conference held on 6 October 1849, he assigned several members of the Twelve, along with newly called missionaries, to serve foreign missions. They accepted these calls even though they would leave behind their families, their new homes, and many unfinished tasks. Erastus Snow and several elders opened missionary work in Scandinavia, while Lorenzo Snow and Joseph Toronto traveled to Italy. Addison and Louisa Barnes Pratt returned to Addison's former field of labor in the Society Islands. John Taylor was called to France and Germany. As the missionaries traveled east, they passed Saints headed to the new Zion in the Rocky Mountains.

In their fields of labor, the missionaries witnessed miracles and baptized many people into the Church. When Lorenzo Snow, who later became President of the Church, was preaching in Italy, he saw a three-year-old boy on the verge of death. He recognized an opportunity to heal the child and open the hearts of the people in the area. That night he prayed long and earnestly for God's direction, and the following day he and his companion fasted and prayed for the boy. That afternoon they administered to him and offered a silent prayer for help in their labors. The boy slept peacefully all night and was miraculously healed. Word of this healing spread across the valleys of the Piedmont in Italy. The doors were opened to the missionaries, and the first baptisms in the area took place.[5]

In August 1852, at a special conference held in Salt Lake City, 106 elders were called to go on missions to countries throughout the world. These missionaries, as well as those who were called later, preached the gospel in South America, China, India, Spain, Australia, Hawaii, and the South Pacific. In most of these areas, the missionaries had little initial success. However, they sowed seeds that resulted in many coming into the Church in later missionary efforts.

Elder Edward Stevenson was called to the Gibraltar Mission in Spain. This call meant a return to the place of his birth, where he boldly proclaimed the restored gospel to his countrymen. He was arrested for preaching and spent some time in jail until authorities found he was teaching the guards, almost converting one of them. After his release he baptized two people into the Church and by January 1854 a branch of ten members had been organized. In July, even though six members had left to serve with the British army in Asia, the branch had eighteen members, including one seventy, one elder, one priest, and one teacher, giving the branch the leadership it needed to continue to grow.[6]

Local governments in French Polynesia drove the missionaries out in 1852. But the converted Saints kept the Church alive until further proselyting efforts in 1892. Elders Tihoni and Maihea were especially valiant as they endured imprisonment and other ordeals rather than deny their faith. Each of them tried to keep the Saints active and faithful to the gospel.[7]

For those who joined the Church outside the United States, this was a time for gathering to Zion, which meant traveling by boat to America. Elizabeth and Charles Wood sailed in 1860 from South Africa, where they had labored several years to acquire money for their travel. Elizabeth kept house for a wealthy man, and her husband made bricks until they obtained the needed funds. Elizabeth was carried aboard the ship on a bed 24 hours after delivering a son and was given the captain's berth so she could be more comfortable. She was very ill during the journey, almost dying twice, but lived to settle in Fillmore, Utah.

Missionaries became very dear to the Saints in the countries where they served. Joseph F. Smith, near the end of his mission to Hawaii in 1857, became ill with a high fever that prevented him from working for three months. He was blessed to come under the care of Ma Mahuhii, a faithful Hawaiian Saint. She nursed Joseph as if he were her own son, and a strong bond of love developed between the two. Years later, when he was President of the Church, Joseph F. Smith visited Honolulu and just after his arrival saw an old blind woman being led in with a few choice bananas in her hand as an offering. He heard her call, "Iosepa, Iosepa" (Joseph, Joseph). Immediately he ran to her and hugged and kissed her many times, patting her on the head and saying, "Mama, Mama, my dear old Mama."[8]

Callings to Colonize

Many communities in Utah and southern Idaho and later in parts of Arizona, Wyoming, Nevada, and California were founded by individuals and families called at general conferences. President Brigham Young directed the establishment of these communities, where thousands of new settlers could live and farm.

During his lifetime, all of the Salt Lake Valley and many surrounding areas were colonized. By 1877, when Brigham Young

Answering calls from President Brigham Young, many Saints left their established homes to colonize new communities.

died, more than 350 colonies had been established, and by 1900 there were almost 500. Early Church authority Brigham Henry Roberts noted that the success of Mormon colonization stemmed from "the loyalty of the people to their leaders and [their] unselfish and devoted personal sacrifice" in carrying out their calls from President Young.[9] The colonists sacrificed material comforts, the associations of friends, and sometimes their lives to follow a prophet of the Lord.

At general conference meetings, President Young read the names of those brethren and their families who were being called to move to outlying areas. These colonizers considered that they were being called on missions and knew that they would remain in their assigned locales until they were released. They traveled to their new areas at their own expense and with their own supplies. Their success depended on how well they used the resources at hand. They surveyed and cleared fields, built gristmills, dug irrigation ditches to bring water to the land, fenced pastures for their stock, and built roads. They planted crops and gardens, built churches and schools, and tried to maintain friendly relations with the Indians. They helped each other in sickness, as well as in births, deaths, and weddings.

In 1862 Charles Lowell Walker received a call to settle in southern Utah. He attended a meeting for those who had been called and recorded: "Here I learned a principle that I shall not forget in awhile. It showed to me that obedience was a great principle in heaven and on earth. Well, here I have worked for the last seven years through heat and cold, hunger and adverse circumstances, and at last have got me a home, a lot with fruit trees just beginning to bear and look pretty. Well, I must leave it and go and do the will of my Father in Heaven, who overrules all for the good of them that love and fear him. I pray God to give me strength to accomplish that which is required of me in an acceptable manner before him."[10]

Charles C. Rich, a member of the Quorum of Twelve Apostles, also received a call to colonize. Brigham Young called him and a

few other brethren to take their families and settle in the Bear
Lake Valley, about 150 miles north of Salt Lake City. The valley
was at a high altitude and was very cold with deep snows in the
winter. Brother Rich had recently returned from a mission in
Europe and was not anxious to move his family and start over
again in difficult circumstances. But he accepted the call and in
June 1864 arrived in the Bear Lake Valley. The next winter was
unusually severe and by spring, some of the other brethren had
decided to leave. Brother Rich realized that life would not be easy
in this cold climate but said:

"There have been many hardships. That I admit . . . and these
we have shared together. But if you want to go somewhere else,
that is your right, and I do not want to deprive you of it. . . . But
I must stay here, even if I stay alone. President Young called me
here, and here I will remain till he releases me and gives me leave
to go." Brother Rich and his family did stay, and he became the
leader of a thriving community for the next several decades.[11] Like
thousands of others, he willingly obeyed his leaders in order to
help build the kingdom of the Lord.

Relations with the Indians

As colonists moved further into the frontier, they often had
dealings with the Indians. Unlike some settlers of the West,
President Brigham Young taught the Saints to feed their native
brothers and sisters and try to bring them into the Church.
Proselyting efforts among the Indians were tried at Fort Lemhi
in the Salmon River region of Idaho Territory and in the Elk
Mountain settlement on the upper Colorado in the Utah Territory.
President Young also instituted Relief Societies whose members
sewed clothing for their Indian brothers and sisters and raised
money to help feed them.

When Elizabeth Kane, who was the wife of Thomas L. Kane,
a great nonmember friend of the Saints, traveled through Utah,
she stayed at the home of a weary Mormon woman. Elizabeth did
not think much of the woman until she saw how she treated the

Indians. When the woman called her guests to supper, she also spoke a few words to the Indians who were waiting. Elizabeth asked what the woman had said to the Indians and a son in the family told her, "These strangers came first, and I have only cooked enough for them; but your meal is on the fire cooking now, and I will call you as soon as it is ready." Elizabeth was unbelieving and asked if she really would feed the Indians. The son told her, "Mother will serve them just as she does you, and give them a place at her table." She did serve them, waiting on them while they ate.[12]

Organization of Priesthood and Auxiliary Functions

In his later years, President Young clarified and established some important priesthood responsibilities. He directed the Twelve to hold conferences in every stake. As a result, seven new stakes and 140 new wards were created throughout Utah. The duties of stake presidencies, high councils, bishoprics, and quorum presidencies were clearly defined, and hundreds of men were called to fill these positions. He counseled Church members to put their lives in order and pay their tithing, fast offerings, and other donations.

In 1867 the prophet appointed George Q. Cannon as general superintendent of the Sunday School, and within a few years, the Sunday School was a permanent part of the Church organization. In 1869 President Young began giving formal instruction in modest living to his daughters. He expanded this counsel to all young women in 1870 with the formation of the Retrenchment Association (*retrench* means to cut back excesses). This was the beginning of the Young Women organization. In July 1877 he traveled to Ogden, Utah, to organize the first stake Relief Society.

President Brigham Young's Death and Legacy

As a leader, President Brigham Young was practical and energetic. He traveled to the settlements of the Church to instruct and encourage the Saints. By direction and example, he taught members to fulfill their callings in the Church.

In evaluating his life, President Young wrote the following in response to an editor of a New York newspaper:

"The result of my labors for the past 26 years, briefly summed up, are: The peopling of this Territory by the Latter-day Saints of about 100,000 souls; the founding of over 200 cities, towns and villages inhabited by our people, . . . and the establishment of schools, factories, mills and other institutions calculated to improve and benefit our communities. . . .

"My whole life is devoted to the Almighty's service."[13]

In September 1876, President Young bore powerful witness of the Savior: "I testify that Jesus is the Christ, the Savior and Redeemer of the world; I have obeyed his sayings, and realized his promise, and the knowledge I have of him, the wisdom of this world cannot give, neither can it take away."[14]

In August 1877, President Young fell very ill, and in spite of physicians' care, died within a week. He was 76 years old and had led the Church for 33 years. Today we remember him as the dynamic prophet who led modern-day Israel to their promised land. His sermons touched on all aspects of daily life, making clear that religion is part of everyday experience. His understanding of the frontier and his sensible guidance inspired his people to accomplish seemingly impossible tasks as with the blessings of heaven they created a kingdom in the desert.

Thousands of Saints gathered to witness the laying of the capstone on the Salt Lake Temple, 6 April 1892.

CHAPTER EIGHT

A Period of Trials and Testing

President John Taylor

After President Brigham Young died, the Quorum of the Twelve Apostles, presided over by John Taylor, led the Latter-day Saints for three years. On 10 October 1880, John Taylor was sustained as President of the Church. President Taylor was a gifted writer and journalist who published a book on the Atonement and edited some of the Church's most important periodicals, including the *Times and Seasons* and the *Mormon*. On many occasions he displayed his courage and his deep devotion to the restored gospel, including voluntarily joining his brethren in Carthage Jail, where he was shot four times. His personal motto, "The kingdom of God or nothing," signified his loyalty to God and the Church.

Missionary Work

President Taylor was committed to doing all he could to see that the gospel was proclaimed to the ends of the earth. In the October 1879 general conference, he called Moses Thatcher, the Church's newest Apostle, to begin proselyting in Mexico City, Mexico. Elder Thatcher and two other missionaries organized the first branch of the Church in Mexico City on 13 November 1879, with Dr. Plotino C. Rhodacanaty as the branch president. Dr. Rhodacanaty had been converted after reading a Spanish Book of Mormon pamphlet and writing to President Taylor for additional information about the Church.

With a nucleus of twelve members and three missionaries, the restored gospel began to spread slowly among the Mexican people.

On 6 April 1881, Elder Thatcher, Feramorz Young, and a Brother Paez hiked to a height of 15,500 feet on Mount Popocatepetl and held a brief dedication service. Kneeling before the Lord, Elder Thatcher dedicated the land of Mexico and its people that they might hear the voice of the Lord, their true shepherd.

Elder Thatcher returned to Salt Lake City and recommended that additional missionaries be called to serve in Mexico. Soon several young men, including Anthony W. Ivins, a future member of the First Presidency, were laboring in Mexico City. As part of the Church's effort in the Mexican Mission, a Spanish language edition of the Book of Mormon was published in 1886. The story of Meliton Trejo, who helped to translate the Book of Mormon and other Church literature into Spanish, demonstrates how the Lord directs his work.

Meliton Trejo was born in Spain and grew up without settling on any religion. He was serving in the military in the Philippines when he heard a remark about the Mormons in the Rocky Mountains and felt a strong desire to visit them. Later he became very ill and was told in a dream that he must visit Utah. When he recovered, he journeyed to Salt Lake City. He met Brigham Young and investigated the gospel. He became convinced that he had found the truth and became a member of the Church. He served a mission in Mexico and was then prepared, spiritually and intellectually, to play a major role in seeing that Spanish-speaking people could read the Book of Mormon in their own language.

President Taylor also called missionaries to carry the gospel to the Indians living in the American West. Amos Wright's labors were particularly fruitful among the Shoshone tribe residing on Wyoming's Wind River Reservation. After having served for only a few months, Wright had baptized more than 300 Indians, including Chief Washakie. Latter-day Saint missionaries also carried the gospel to the Navajos, the Pueblos, and the Zunis living in Arizona and New Mexico. Wilford Woodruff spent a year proselyting among the Indians, including the Hopis, Apaches, and

Zunis. Ammon M. Tenney assisted in baptizing more than 100 Zuni Indians.

Missionaries also continued to teach the gospel in England and Europe. In 1883, German-born Thomas Biesinger, who was living in Lehi, Utah, received a call to serve in the European mission. He and Paul Hammer were sent to Prague, Czechoslovakia, then part of the Austro-Hungarian empire. The missionaries were forbidden by law to proselyte and so initiated casual conversations with people they met. These conversations often turned to the subject of religion. After working in this way for only a month, Elder Biesinger was arrested and held in prison for two months. When he gained his freedom, he had the blessing of baptizing Antonín Just, whose accusation had led to his arrest. Brother Just became the first Latter-day Saint residing in Czechoslovakia.[1]

The gospel was also preached in Polynesia. Two Hawaiians, Elders Kimo Pelio and Samuela Manoa, were sent to Samoa in 1862. They baptized about 50 people, and Elder Manoa continued to live in Samoa with his converts for the next 25 years. In 1887 Joseph H. Dean of Salt Lake City, Utah, received a call to serve a mission in Samoa. Elder Manoa and his faithful wife opened their home to Elder Dean and his wife, Florence, the first Latter-day Saints from outside Samoa they had seen in more than two decades. Elder Dean soon baptized 14 people into the Church and about a month later delivered his first sermon in the Samoan language.[2] Thus missionary work began anew on the island.

Beginning in 1866, to prevent the spread of leprosy, Hawaiian officials took people suffering from the disease to the Kalaupapa Peninsula on the island of Molokai. In 1873 Jonathan and Kitty Napela, who were Latter-day Saints, were banished there. Only Kitty had the disease, but Jonathan, who had been sealed to her in the Salt Lake Endowment House, would not leave her there alone. Jonathan later contracted the disease, and when he was visited nine years later by a good friend, was hardly recognizable. For some time he presided over the Saints on the peninsula, who by the year 1900 numbered more than 200. Church leaders did not forget the faithful members who suffered from this debilitating disease and frequently visited the branch to care for their spiritual needs.[3]

The Jubilee Conference

On 6 April 1880, Church members celebrated the fiftieth anniversary of the organization of the Church. They called it a Jubilee Year, as the ancient Israelites had named every fiftieth year. President Taylor forgave many of the debts owed to the Church by its needy members. The Church also contributed 300 cows and 2,000 sheep to be distributed among its "deserving poor."[4] The Church's Relief Society sisters donated almost 35,000 bushels of wheat to those in need. President Taylor also urged Church members to forgive individual debt, especially among the distressed. "It is the time of Jubilee!" he declared.[5] A spirit of forgiveness and joy was strongly felt among the Latter-day Saints.

The last day of the April 1880 Jubilee general conference was very moving. Eleven of the Twelve Apostles bore their testimonies in the concluding session. Orson Pratt, one of the original members of the Quorum of the Twelve Apostles, spoke about the time when the entire Church had met in the Peter Whitmer Sr. home in Fayette, New York. He recalled the trials, the gatherings, the persecutions, and the afflictions of the Latter-day Saints and felt thankful that he was still "numbered with this people." Then he bore testimony "concerning the great work which the Lord our God has been doing during the last fifty years."[6] Elder Pratt had only a few months left to live and felt joyful that he had endured to the end as a faithful Latter-day Saint.

Two years before the Jubilee celebration, President John Taylor had authorized the establishment of an organization to provide religious instruction to children. The first Primary was begun in Farmington, Utah, about 15 miles north of Salt Lake City, and by the mid-1880s, a Primary had been organized in almost all Latter-day Saint settlements. The Primary has grown to include millions of children throughout the world, who are blessed by the gospel instruction, music, and associations they enjoy each week.

Persecution Continues

While working on the translation of the Bible in the early 1830s, the Prophet Joseph Smith became troubled by the fact that Abraham, Jacob, David, and other Old Testament leaders had more than one wife. The Prophet prayed for understanding and learned that at certain times, for specific purposes, following divinely given laws, plural marriage was approved and directed by God. Joseph Smith also learned that with divine approval, some Latter-day Saints would soon be chosen by priesthood authority to marry more than one wife. A number of Latter-day Saints practiced plural marriage in Nauvoo, but a public announcement of this doctrine and practice was not made until the August 1852 general conference in Salt Lake City. At that conference, Elder Orson Pratt, as directed by President Brigham Young, announced that the practice of a man having more than one wife was part of the Lord's restitution of all things (see Acts 3:19–21).

Many of America's religious and political leaders became very angry when they learned that Latter-day Saints living in Utah were encouraging a marriage system that they considered immoral and unchristian. A great political crusade was launched against the Church and its members. The United States Congress passed legislation that curbed the freedom of the Latter-day Saints and hurt the Church economically. This legislation ultimately caused officers to arrest and imprison men who had more than one wife and to deny them the right to vote, the right to privacy in their homes, and the enjoyment of other civil liberties. Hundreds of faithful Latter-day Saint men and a few women served time in prisons located in Utah, Idaho, Arizona, Nebraska, Michigan, and South Dakota.

Persecution also became intense for many who accepted callings to preach the gospel, especially in the southern United States. For example, in July 1878 Elder Joseph Standing was brutally murdered while laboring near Rome, Georgia. His companion, the future Apostle Rudger Clawson, only narrowly escaped death. The Saints in Salt Lake City were very affected by the news of

Elder Standing's murder, and thousands of people attended his funeral in the Salt Lake Tabernacle.

Elders John Gibbs, William Berry, William Jones, and Henry Thompson traveled throughout much of Tennessee attempting to change the public's perception of the Church. They rested one Sabbath morning in August 1884 at the James Condor home near Cane Creek in Tennessee. As Elder Gibbs studied the scriptures looking for a text for his sermon, a mob burst through the forest and began shooting. Elders Gibbs and Berry were killed. Elder Gibbs, a schoolteacher, left a wife and three children mourning his death. Sister Gibbs remained a widow for 43 years and became a midwife to support her children. She died faithful in the gospel, anticipating a joyful reunion with her husband. Brigham Henry Roberts, the acting mission president at the time of the murders, risked his life by going in disguise to exhume the bodies of Gibbs and Berry. He returned the bodies to Utah, where many wards held memorial services in honor of the two elders.

Missionaries in other areas were beaten until blood ran down their backs, and many carried the scars of these whippings to their graves. It was not an easy time to be a member of the Church.

Many Church leaders went into hiding to avoid arrest by federal officers searching for men with more than one wife. Families feared late-night intrusions by these officers. President George Q. Cannon, Lorenzo Snow, Rudger Clawson, Brigham Henry Roberts, George Reynolds, and many others were sent to prison, where they passed the time by writing books, teaching school, and composing letters to their families. President John Taylor was forced to live in exile in Kaysville, Utah, about 20 miles north of Salt Lake City, where he died on 25 July 1887. He was a man of faith and courage who devoted his life to his testimony of Jesus Christ and to the establishment of God's kingdom on the earth.

President Wilford Woodruff

Wilford Woodruff was one of the Church's most successful missionaries and was also known for his prophetic insights and loyalty to the Church. He kept meticulous journals, which provide much information about the early history of the Church. He was serving as President of the Quorum of the Twelve Apostles when John Taylor died, and almost two years later he was sustained as the President of the Church.

During his administration, the political crusade against the Latter-day Saints intensified, but the Church moved forward. Temples were operating in three Utah towns—St. George, Logan, and Manti—and the Salt Lake Temple was nearing completion. These houses of the Lord enabled thousands of Saints to obtain their endowments and do ordinance work for their kindred dead. President Woodruff had a lifelong interest in temple and family history work. He admonished the Saints on many occasions to perform ordinances in the temple for their ancestors.

The following incident emphasizes the importance of the work the Saints were performing for the dead. In May 1884, Bishop Henry Ballard of the Logan Second Ward was signing temple recommends at his home. Henry's nine-year-old daughter, who was talking with friends on the sidewalk near her home, saw two elderly men approaching. They called to her, handed her a newspaper, and told her to take it to her father.

The girl did as she was asked. Bishop Ballard saw that the paper, the *Newbury Weekly News*, published in England, contained the names of more than 60 of his and his father's acquaintances, along with genealogical information. This newspaper, dated 15 May 1884, had been given to him only three days after it was printed. In a time long before air transportation, when mail took several weeks to get from England to western America, this was a miracle.

The next day, Bishop Ballard took the newspaper to the temple and told the story of its arrival to Marriner W. Merrill, the temple president. President Merrill declared, "Brother Ballard, someone on the other side is anxious for their work to be done and they knew that you would do it if this paper got into your hands."[7] This newspaper is preserved in the Church Historical Library in Salt Lake City, Utah.

In spite of persecution, Church leaders still encouraged the colonization of unsettled areas in America's west. Beginning in 1885, many Latter-day Saint families settled in Sonora and Chihuahua, Mexico, establishing such towns as Colonia Juárez and Colonia Díaz. Other areas in northern Mexico also received immigrant Church members.

Church members also looked north to Canada for a place to colonize. Charles O. Card, who served as president of the Cache Valley Stake, founded a Latter-day Saint community in southern Alberta in 1886. By the winter of 1888, more than 100 Latter-day Saints lived in western Canada, and more came during the 1890s, providing the labor to construct an irrigation system and a railroad. Many Church leaders matured in Alberta.

The Manifesto

As the 1880s drew to a close, the United States government passed additional laws that deprived those who practiced plural marriage of the right to vote and serve on juries and severely restricted the amount of property the Church could own. Latter-day Saint families suffered as even more fathers went into hiding. President Woodruff pleaded with the Lord for guidance. On the evening of 23 September 1890, the prophet, acting under inspiration, wrote the Manifesto, a document that ended plural marriage for Church members. The Lord showed President Woodruff in vision that unless the practice of plural marriage was ended, the United States government would take over the temples, thus ending work for the living and the dead.

On 24 September 1890, the First Presidency and the Quorum of Twelve Apostles sustained the Manifesto. The Saints approved it in the October 1890 general conference. Today this document is included in the Doctrine and Covenants as Official Declaration 1.

Following the Church's action, federal officials issued pardons to Latter-day Saint men convicted of violating the antipolygamy laws and much of the persecution stopped. But, as President Woodruff explained: "I should have let all the temples go out of our hands; I should have gone to prison myself, and let every other man go there, had not the God of heaven commanded me to do what I did do; and when the hour came that I was commanded to do that, it was all clear to me. I went before the Lord, and I wrote what the Lord told me to write" ("Excerpts from Three Addresses by President Wilford Woodruff Regarding the Manifesto," included after Official Declaration 1). God, not the United States Congress, brought about the official discontinuance of plural marriage.

The Genealogical Society

Long before the Latter-day Saints founded a genealogical society, Church members gathered records documenting the lives of their dead ancestors. Wilford Woodruff, Orson Pratt, and Heber J. Grant are among those who obtained the names of thousands of ancestors for whom they performed temple ordinances. In 1894, the First Presidency directed that a genealogical society be organized with Elder Franklin D. Richards as its first leader. A library was established, and representatives of the society went throughout the world in search of names of people for whom temple ordinances could be performed. This society led to the creation of the Family History Department of the Church.

During the April 1894 general conference, President Woodruff announced that he had received a revelation about genealogical work. He declared that God wanted the Latter-day Saints "to trace their genealogies as far as they can, and to be sealed to their fathers and mothers. Have the children sealed to their parents and run this chain through as far as you can get it. . . . This is the will of the Lord to his people," he said, "and I think when you come to reflect upon it you will find it to be true."[8] Latter-day Saints are still encouraged to seek out the records of their deceased ancestors and perform temple ordinances in their behalf.

From 1885 to 1900, many Church members served genealogical missions. They were invited to Salt Lake City to receive a blessing for their mission from a General Authority. They were also provided with a missionary card and a letter of appointment. They visited relatives, recorded names from gravestones, and studied parish records and family Bibles, returning to their homes with valuable information that allowed temple work to be performed. Many missionaries reported spiritual experiences that gave them the firm assurance that the Lord was with them and often directed them to a needed source or relative.[9]

Dedication of the Salt Lake Temple

President Wilford Woodruff devoted much of his life to temple work. He was the first president of the St. George Temple, and he dedicated the Manti Temple. Now, 40 years after the cornerstone of the Salt Lake Temple was laid, President Woodruff awaited with great anticipation the dedication of this landmark temple. Dedicatory services were held from 6 April to 18 May 1893, and approximately 75,000 people attended.[10]

Following the initial dedicatory service on 6 April, President Woodruff wrote in his journal: "The spirit and power of God rested upon us. The spirit of prophecy and revelation was upon us and the hearts of the people were melted and many things were unfolded to us."[11] Some Latter-day Saints saw angels, while others saw past Presidents of the Church and other deceased Church leaders.[12]

When President Woodruff celebrated his ninetieth birthday, thousands of Sunday School children filled the Tabernacle on Temple Square to honor him. He was deeply moved and, speaking with great emotion, told his young audience that when he was ten years of age he attended a Protestant Sunday School and read about apostles and prophets. When he returned home, he prayed that he might live long enough to see apostles and prophets once more on the earth. Now he stood in the presence of men who were both apostles and prophets; his prayer had been answered many times over.[13]

A year later on 2 September 1898, President Woodruff died while visiting in San Francisco.

President Lorenzo Snow and Tithing

After the death of President Woodruff, Lorenzo Snow, President of the Quorum of the Twelve, became President of the Church. He was a wise and loving leader who had been prepared well for his responsibilities. He had known and been taught by every latter-day prophet up to that time. In November 1900, he told the Saints assembled in the Tabernacle that he had often visited the Prophet Joseph Smith and his family, dined at his table, and had private interviews with him. He knew Joseph was a prophet of God because the Lord had shown him this truth "most clearly and completely."[14]

During President Snow's administration, the Church faced serious financial difficulties that had been brought about by the federal government's legislation against plural marriage. President Snow pondered and prayed for guidance about how to free the Church from its debilitating debt. Following the April 1899 general conference, he felt inspired to visit St. George, Utah. While speaking at a meeting there he paused for some time, and when he continued, he declared that he had received a revelation. The people of the Church had neglected the law of tithing, and the Lord had told him that if Church members more faithfully paid a full tithing, blessings would be showered upon them.

The prophet preached the importance of tithing to congregations throughout Utah. The Saints obeyed his counsel, and that year they paid twice as much tithing as the previous year. By 1907, the Church possessed sufficient funds to pay all its creditors and become debt-free.

In 1898, at a reception for the general board of the Young Ladies Mutual Improvement Association, President George Q. Cannon announced that the First Presidency had made a decision to call "some of our wise and prudent women into the missionary field."[15] Before this time, a few sisters had accompanied their husbands on missions, but this was the first time that the Church had officially called and set apart sisters as missionary ambassadors of the Lord Jesus Christ. While sisters do not have the duty to serve missions, in the past decades thousands have exercised this privilege and served the Lord valiantly as full-time missionaries.

President Lorenzo Snow led the Church into the twentieth century. When the new century dawned, the Church had 43 stakes, 20 missions, and 967 wards and branches. There were 283,765 members, most of whom resided in the Rocky Mountain area of the United States. Four temples were in operation, and the *Juvenile Instructor, Improvement Era,* and *Young Women's Journal* carried articles about the Church to its members. Rumors circulated that at least one new mission might be opened, and Latter-day Saints could scarcely imagine what the next hundred years would bring. Yet they were confident that prophecies concerning the destiny of the Church would be fulfilled.

CHAPTER NINE

The Expanding Church

From 1901 to 1970, four prophets presided over an expanding Church—Joseph F. Smith, Heber J. Grant, George Albert Smith, and David O. McKay. These Presidents witnessed the transition from horse and buggy transportation to travel by rocket into outer space. Two world wars and a global depression challenged the Saints. During this time, nine temples were built. In 1901, there were approximately 300,000 members in 50 stakes, and by 1970 the Church had over 2,800,000 members gathered in 500 stakes throughout the world.

President Joseph F. Smith

Joseph F. Smith was born in 1838 during the height of the Missouri persecutions in a small cabin near the temple site in Far West. At the time of Joseph's birth, his father, Hyrum Smith, was imprisoned at Richmond, Missouri, and his mother, Mary Fielding Smith, was left alone to care for her children.

Young Joseph moved with his family from Missouri to Nauvoo, Illinois, where an event occurred that he remembered for the rest of his life—the murder of his father and uncle at Carthage Jail. Joseph never forgot seeing his father for the last time when, on the way to Carthage on horseback, he picked up his son, kissed him, and set him down. Nor could he forget the terror of hearing a neighbor rap on the window at night to tell his mother that Hyrum had been killed. The sight of his father and uncle lying in their coffins in the Mansion House in Nauvoo never faded from his memory.

The boy Joseph became a man almost overnight. When Mary Fielding Smith and her family joined the exodus from Nauvoo,

7-year-old Joseph was the teamster of one of her wagons. Joseph was 13 when his mother died, leaving him an orphan, and before he turned 16, he left on a mission to the Sandwich Islands (later called the Hawaiian Islands). Within three months after arriving in Honolulu, he spoke the native tongue fluently, a spiritual gift conferred upon him by Elders Parley P. Pratt and Orson Hyde of the Twelve, who set him apart. When he was 21, he left for another mission, this time for three years in the British Isles.

Joseph was only 28 when President Brigham Young was impressed to ordain him an Apostle. In subsequent years he served as a Counselor to four Church Presidents. When Lorenzo Snow died in October 1901, Joseph F. Smith became the sixth President of the Church. He was well known for his ability to expound and defend gospel truths. His sermons and writings were compiled into a volume titled *Gospel Doctrine,* which has become one of the important doctrinal texts of the Church.

In the opening decades of the twentieth century, the Church moved forward in several important ways. With the continued emphasis on tithing and the Saints' faithful response, the Church was able to pay off all its debts. A period of prosperity followed, enabling the Church to build temples, chapels, and visitors' centers and to purchase Church historical sites. The Church also built the Administration Building in Salt Lake City that still serves as its headquarters.

President Smith recognized the need for temples throughout the world. At a 1906 conference in Bern, Switzerland, he stretched out his hand and declared, "The time will come when this land will be dotted with temples, where you can go and redeem your dead."[1] The first latter-day temple in Europe, the Swiss Temple, was dedicated nearly half a century later in a suburb of the city where President Smith made his prophecy. President Smith dedicated land for a temple in Cardston, Alberta, Canada, in 1913 and for a temple in Hawaii in 1915.

Beginning in the early 1900s, Church leaders encouraged Saints to remain in their own lands rather than gather to Utah.

In 1911 Joseph F. Smith and his Counselors in the First Presidency issued this statement: "It is desirable that our people shall remain in their native lands and form congregations of a permanent character to aid in the work of proselyting."[2]

Six weeks before President Smith died, he received an important revelation about the redemption of the dead. He saw in vision the Savior's ministry in the spirit world and learned that faithful Saints have the opportunity to continue teaching the gospel in the world of spirits. This revelation was added to the Pearl of Great Price in 1976 and in 1979 was transferred to the Doctrine and Covenants as section 138.

President Heber J. Grant

Shortly before his death in November 1918, President Joseph F. Smith took Heber J. Grant, then President of the Twelve, by the hand and said: "The Lord bless you, my boy, the Lord bless you, you have got a great responsibility. Always remember that this is the Lord's work, and not man's. The Lord is greater than any man. He knows whom He wants to lead His Church, and never makes any mistake."[3] Heber J. Grant became the seventh President of the Church at age 62, having served as an Apostle since 1882.

As a young man and throughout his life, Heber showed an unusual determination in achieving his goals. As an only child reared by a widowed mother, he was somewhat sheltered from the activities of other boys his age. When he tried out for the baseball team, he was teased for his awkwardness and lack of skill and was not accepted as a team member. Instead of becoming discouraged, he spent many hours of persistent practice in throwing a ball and eventually became a member of another team that won several local championships.

As a boy he wanted to become a bookkeeper when he learned that it would pay much more than his job of shining shoes. In those days, being a bookkeeper required good penmanship skills, but his writing was so bad that two of his friends said it looked like hen tracks. Once again, he was not discouraged but spent

The Church established welfare farms to help provide food for the needy. Church members contributed their labor, as illustrated by these Saints working on a sugar beet farm in 1933.

many hours practicing his penmanship. He became well known for his ability to write beautifully, eventually taught penmanship at a university, and was often called on to write important documents. He was a great example to many people who saw his determination to do the best he could in serving the Lord and his fellowmen.

President Grant was a wise and successful businessman whose skills helped him lead the Church through a worldwide financial depression and the personal problems that resulted from it. He firmly believed in being self-reliant and in depending on the Lord and his own hard work, not on the government. He blessed many needy people with the money he earned.

In the 1930s the Saints, like many other people in the world, were struggling with unemployment and poverty during the Great Depression. In 1936, as a result of revelation from the Lord,

President Grant established the welfare program of the Church to assist those in need and help all members become self-reliant. The First Presidency said of this program: "Our primary purpose was to set up, in so far as it might be possible, a system under which the curse of idleness would be done away with, the evils of a dole abolished, and independence, industry, thrift and self respect be once more established amongst our people. The aim of the Church is to help the people to help themselves. Work is to be re-enthroned as the ruling principle of the lives of our Church membership."[4]

President J. Reuben Clark Jr., who served as a Counselor in the First Presidency for 28 years, emphasized, "The real long term objective of the Welfare Plan is the building of character in the members of the Church, givers and receivers, rescuing all that is finest down deep inside of them, and bringing to flower and fruitage the latent richness of the spirit."[5]

A General Welfare Committee was established in 1936 to oversee welfare efforts in the Church. Harold B. Lee, president of the Pioneer Stake, was made the committee's managing director. Later, Deseret Industries stores were developed to help the unemployed and handicapped, and farms and production projects were established to help the needy. The welfare program continues to bless thousands of people today, both needy Church members and others in destitute circumstances throughout the world.[6]

While missionary work continued at an expanded pace, President Grant was instrumental in a most unusual conversion. Vincenzo di Francesca, an Italian minister of religion, was walking down a New York City street toward his church when he saw a book without a cover in a barrel full of ashes. He picked up the book, turned the pages, and saw for the first time the names Nephi, Mosiah, Alma, and Moroni. He felt impressed to read the book even though he did not know its name or origin, and to pray about its truthfulness. As he did, he said that "a feeling of gladness, as of finding something precious and extraordinary, bore consolation to my soul and left me with a joy that human language cannot find words to describe." He began teaching the principles in the book to the members of his church. His church leaders disciplined him for doing so and even directed him to burn the book, something he refused to do.

He later returned to Italy, where in 1930 he learned that the book was published by The Church of Jesus Christ of Latter-day Saints. He wrote a letter to the Church in Utah that was forwarded to President Grant. President Grant sent him a copy of the Book of Mormon in Italian and gave his name to the president of the European mission. The difficulties of wartime prevented Vincenzo from being baptized for many years, but he was finally able to become a member of the Church on 18 January 1951, the first person baptized on the island of Sicily. Five years later he was endowed in the Swiss Temple.[7]

On 6 May 1922 President Grant dedicated the Church's first radio station. Two years later the station began broadcasting sessions of general conference, allowing many more Church members to hear the messages of the General Authorities. Not long thereafter, in July of 1929, the Tabernacle Choir aired the first program of *Music and the Spoken Word*, a weekly broadcast of inspirational music and spoken message. This program has continued to be broadcast each week to the present time.

President Grant died on 14 May 1945. His 27 years of service as President of the Church are exceeded in length only by Brigham Young's years of service.

President George Albert Smith

George Albert Smith succeeded Heber J. Grant as Church President. President Smith, whose life was an example of the happiness found in gospel living, testified: "Every happiness and every joy that has been worthy of the name has been the result of keeping the commandments of God and observing his advice and counsel."[8]

Obeying the commandments of God and the counsel of Church leaders had been a pattern of righteousness in President

Smith's family for generations. He was named for his paternal grandfather, George A. Smith, who was a cousin to the Prophet Joseph and a Counselor to President Brigham Young. George Albert's father, John Henry Smith, served in the First Presidency under Joseph F. Smith. At the age of 33, George Albert Smith was called to the Quorum of the Twelve. From 1903 to 1910, John Henry and George Albert served together in the Quorum of the Twelve, the only time in this dispensation that a father and son have served together in that Quorum.

George Albert Smith's 42 years in the Quorum of the Twelve were filled with noble service, despite episodes of poor health. His eyes were damaged by the sun while surveying for the railroad in southern Utah, and surgery failed to correct his near blindness. Increased pressures and demands on his time weakened his frail body, and in 1909 he collapsed from exhaustion. The doctor's order of complete rest eroded his self-confidence, created feelings of worthlessness, and aggravated his tension.

During this difficult time, George had a dream in which he saw a beautiful forest near a large lake. After he had walked some distance through the forest, he recognized his beloved grandfather, George A. Smith, coming toward him. George hurried forward, but as his grandfather drew near, he stopped and said, "I would like to know what you have done with my name." A panorama of his life passed through George's mind and he humbly replied, "I have never done anything with your name of which you need be ashamed." This dream renewed George's spirit and physical stamina and he was soon able to return to work. Later he often described the experience as a major turning point in his life.[9]

During President George Albert Smith's administration, which lasted from 1945 to 1951, the number of members in the Church reached one million; the temple in Idaho Falls, Idaho, was dedicated; and missionary work was resumed after World War II.

Also, efforts were organized for relief of the European Saints who had become destitute as a result of the war. Church members in the United States were encouraged to contribute clothing and other commodities. President Smith met with Harry S. Truman, president of the United States, to receive approval to send the collected food, clothing, and bedding to Europe. President Smith described the meeting in this way:

President Truman said: " 'What do you want to ship it over there for? Their money isn't any good.'

"I said, 'We don't want their money.' He looked at me and asked: 'You don't mean you are going to give it to them?'

"I said: 'Of course, we would give it to them. They are our brothers and sisters and are in distress. God has blessed us with a surplus, and we will be glad to send it if we can have the co-operation of the government.'

"He said: 'You are on the right track,' and added, 'we will be glad to help you in any way we can.' "[10]

While the donations were being sorted and packaged in Utah to ship overseas, President Smith came to observe the preparations. Tears ran down his face when he saw the great volume of commodities that had been so generously contributed. After a few minutes he removed his new overcoat and said, "Please ship this." Although several people standing nearby told him that he needed his coat on the cold wintry day, he insisted that it be sent.[11]

Elder Ezra Taft Benson of the Quorum of the Twelve was assigned to reopen the missions in Europe, see to the distribution of relief supplies, and administer to the spiritual needs of the Saints. One of Elder Benson's early visits was to a conference of the Saints in Karlsruhe, a German city on the Rhine River. Elder Benson said of the experience:

"We finally found our way to the meeting place, a partially bombed-out building located in the interior of a block. The Saints had been in session for some two hours waiting for us, hoping that we would come because the word had reached them that we might be there for the conference. And then for the first time in my life I saw almost an entire audience in tears as we walked up onto the platform, and they realized that at last, after six or seven long years, representatives from Zion, as they put it, had finally

President Cornelius Zappey and missionaries in the Netherlands Mission handling welfare potatoes for German Saints, 1947

come back to them. . . . As I looked into their upturned faces, pale, thin, many of these Saints dressed in rags, some of them barefooted, I could see the light of faith in their eyes as they bore testimony to the divinity of this great latter-day work, and expressed their gratitude for the blessings of the Lord."[12]

Among his many responsibilities, Elder Benson supervised the distribution of 127 railroad carloads of food, clothing, bedding, and medicine throughout Europe. Years later when President Thomas S. Monson was dedicating a new chapel in Zwickau, Germany, an older brother came forward with tears in his eyes and asked to be remembered to President Ezra Taft Benson. He said to "tell him he saved my life, and those of scores of my brothers and sisters in my native land because of the food and clothing he brought to us from members of the Church in America."[13]

The Dutch Saints had the opportunity to give true Christian service to the starving Saints in Germany. The Dutch members had suffered much during the war and then had received welfare assistance from Church members in the United States. In the spring of 1947, they were asked to begin welfare projects of their own, which they enthusiastically did. They primarily planted potatoes and were expecting a large harvest.

During this time, President Walter Stover of the East German Mission came to Holland and, with tears in his eyes, told of the hunger and desolation of the Church members in Germany. President Cornelius Zappey, the president of the Netherlands Mission, asked his members whether they would supply their growing potatoes to the Germans, who had been their enemies during the war. The members willingly agreed and began to watch their potato crops with increased interest. The harvest was far greater than anyone had expected, and the Dutch Saints were able to send 75 tons of potatoes to their brothers and sisters in Germany. One year later, the Dutch Saints sent 90 tons of potatoes and 9 tons of herring to the Saints in Germany.[14]

The outpouring of Christlike love shown by these Saints was typical of President George Albert Smith, who radiated the love of Christ to an extraordinary extent. He said, "I can say to you, my brethren and sisters, the happiest people in this world are those who love their neighbors as themselves and manifest their appreciation of God's blessings by their conduct in life."[15]

President David O. McKay

David O. McKay was a Counselor to President George Albert Smith in the First Presidency. In the spring of 1951, when it appeared that President Smith's health had become somewhat better, President McKay and his wife, Emma Rae, decided to leave Salt Lake City for their postponed California vacation. They stopped in St. George, Utah, to spend the night. When President McKay awoke early the next morning, he had the distinct impression that he should return to Church headquarters. Within days after he arrived in Salt Lake City, President Smith suffered a stroke that led to his death on 4 April 1951. David O. McKay then became the Church's ninth President.

President David O. McKay as a young boy with his family.
David is on his father's lap.

President McKay had been well prepared to lead the Church. As a child of eight years, he assumed the responsibilities of man of the house when his father was called on a mission to the British Isles. Two of his older sisters had just recently died, his mother was expecting another baby, and his father felt that the responsibilities of the farm were too great to be left to David's mother. Under these circumstances Brother McKay told his wife, "Of course it is impossible for me to go." Sister McKay looked at him and said, "Of course you must accept; you need not worry about me. David O. and I will manage things nicely!"[16] The faith and dedication of his parents implanted in young David a desire to serve the Lord throughout his life. He was called to the Council of the Twelve in 1906 at the age of 32, and he served in that Council and in the First Presidency (as Counselor to President Heber J. Grant and President George Albert Smith) for 45 years before becoming President of the Church.

President McKay began an extensive travel schedule that took him to visit members of a Church that had become worldwide. He visited Saints in Great Britain and Europe, South Africa, Latin

America, the South Pacific, and other places. While he was in Europe, he made preliminary arrangements for the construction of temples in London and Switzerland. Before his Presidency ended, he had visited almost the entire world, blessing and inspiring members of the Church.

President McKay gave renewed emphasis to missionary work by urging every member to make a commitment to bring at least one new member into the Church each year. He became well known for his repeated admonition: "Every member a missionary."

In 1952, in an effort to increase the effectiveness of full-time missionaries, the first official proselyting plan was sent to missionaries throughout the world. It was titled *A Systematic Program for Teaching the Gospel*. It included seven missionary discussions that emphasized teaching by the Spirit and taught clearly the nature of the Godhead, the plan of salvation, the Apostasy and Restoration, and the importance of the Book of Mormon. The number of people converted to the Church throughout the world increased dramatically. In 1961 Church leaders convened the first seminar for all mission presidents, who were taught to encourage families to fellowship their friends and neighbors and then have these people taught by missionaries in their homes. A language training program for newly called missionaries was established in 1961, and later a missionary training center was constructed.

During President McKay's administration, the seeds for the growth of the Church in Asia were planted by Church members serving in the armed forces. A young private from American Fork, Utah, serving in South Korea, noticed that United States soldiers who met Korean civilians made the Koreans jump aside off the path while the soldiers passed by. The young Church member, in contrast, moved aside and let the Koreans use the paths. He also made an effort to learn their names and greeted them pleasantly as he passed by. One day he entered the mess hall with five of his friends. The line to get the food was very long, so he waited at a table for a time. Soon a Korean worker appeared with a tray of food. Pointing to the one stripe on his arm, the soldier said, "You can't serve me. I'm only a private." The Korean replied, "I serve you. You Number One Christian."[17]

By 1967 missionaries and servicemen had been so effective in teaching the gospel in Korea that the Book of Mormon was translated into the Korean language and stakes and wards soon dotted that land.

Missionaries also had great success in Japan. After World War II, Church members in Japan had infrequent contact with Church representatives for several years. But Latter-day Saint servicemen stationed in Japan after the war helped the Church to grow stronger. In 1945, Tatsui Sato was impressed by Latter-day Saint servicemen who declined to drink tea, and he asked them questions that led to his baptism and the baptisms of several of his family members the following year. Elliot Richards baptized Tatsui, and Boyd K. Packer, a serviceman who would later become a member of the Quorum of the Twelve, baptized Sister Sato. The Sato home served as the place where many Japanese people first heard the message of the restored gospel. Soon Latter-day Saint missionaries who had fought against the Japanese during World War II were opening Japanese cities to missionary work.

While the Church presence in the Philippines can also be traced to the efforts of American servicemen and others after World War II, the strong growth of the Church began there in 1961. A young Filipino woman who was not a member of the Church heard about the Book of Mormon and met several Latter-day Saints. As a result, she felt impressed to approach government officials with whom she was acquainted to ask that approval be given for Latter-day Saint missionaries to come to the Philippines. The approval was given and just months later, Elder Gordon B. Hinckley of the Quorum of the Twelve rededicated the country for missionary work.

As a result of the Church's dramatic growth during the 1950s, President McKay announced the priesthood correlation program. A committee, chaired by Elder Harold B. Lee of the Quorum of the

Twelve, was assigned to conduct a thorough, prayerful study of all Church programs to see how well they met the Church's most important objectives. In 1961, with First Presidency approval, Elder Lee announced that policies would be developed to govern the planning, writing, and implementation of all Church curriculum materials. Many of these materials had previously been developed by the Church's auxiliary organizations. This new direction would avoid unnecessary duplication of programs and lesson materials so that the gospel could be more effectively taught to members of all ages and languages in a worldwide Church.

The Church also made other changes in order to more effectively correlate all programs and activities—including welfare, missionary, and family history work—to better accomplish the Church's mission. Home teaching, which had been part of the Church since the time of Joseph Smith, was reemphasized in the 1960s as a way to help care for the spiritual and temporal needs of all Church members. Meetinghouse libraries were established to enhance teaching, and a teacher development program was also put in place. In 1971 the Church began publishing three English-language magazines under General Authority supervision: the *Friend* for children, the *New Era* for young people, and the *Ensign* for adults. At about this same time, the Church unified its foreign language magazines that had previously been published independently by various missions. One magazine is now translated into many languages and sent to Church members throughout the world.

President David O. McKay had long emphasized the importance of home and family life as the source of happiness and the surest defense against the trials and temptations of modern life. He often spoke about the love he felt for his family and the unfailing support he received from his wife, Emma Rae. During President McKay's administration, the practice of holding weekly family home evenings was strongly reemphasized as a way for parents to draw their children closer to them and teach them the principles of the gospel.

The Relief Society supported the prophet in emphasizing the importance of strengthening homes and families. From its beginnings in Nauvoo, the Relief Society had grown to include hundreds of thousands of women throughout the world, who were blessed personally and in their families by the teaching and associations they received through Relief Society. From 1945 to 1974, the general president of the Relief Society was President Belle S. Spafford, a capable leader who also received national recognition when she served as the president of the United States National Council of Women from 1968 to 1970.

President McKay died in January 1970 at age 96. He had presided over the Church for almost 20 years, during which time the membership of the Church increased almost threefold and great strides were made in taking the message of the gospel to the entire world.

Latter-day Saints from around the world rejoice in the blessings of the gospel.

CHAPTER TEN

The Worldwide Church

President Joseph Fielding Smith

When David O. McKay died, President Joseph Fielding Smith, then nearly 93 years of age, became President of the Church. He was the son of former Church President Joseph F. Smith.

As a boy, Joseph Fielding Smith desired to learn the will of the Lord, which prompted him to read the Book of Mormon twice before he was ten years old and to carry the scriptures with him when he walked. When the ball team missed him, they usually found him in the hayloft reading the scriptures. He later said, "From my earliest recollection, from the time I first could read, I have received more pleasure and greater satisfaction out of the study of the scriptures, and reading of the Lord Jesus Christ, and of the Prophet Joseph Smith, and the work that has been accomplished for the salvation of men, than from anything else in all the world."[1]

This early study laid the foundation for an extensive knowledge of the scriptures and Church history, which he drew upon in sermons and in the writing of almost two dozen books and scores of important articles on doctrinal subjects.

During his administration, the first stakes were organized in Asia (Tokyo, Japan) and in Africa (Johannesburg, South Africa). With the growth in Church membership, President Smith and his Counselors began the practice of holding area conferences throughout the world to train local leaders and allow members to meet General Authorities. The first such conference was held in Manchester, England. In order to better serve people throughout the world, health care missionaries were called to teach basic

The first area conference of the Church was held in England in August 1971 under the direction of President Joseph Fielding Smith. Elder Howard W. Hunter is at the podium.

health principles and sanitation. Soon more than 200 health missionaries were serving in many countries.

Since 1912, the Church had sponsored seminary classes in buildings adjacent to high schools in the western United States. In the 1920s, institutes of religion were begun at colleges and universities attended by large numbers of Latter-day Saints. In the early 1950s, early morning seminary classes were started in the Los Angeles, California, area, and soon more than 1,800 students were attending. Nonmember observers were surprised that 15- to 18-year-old Latter-day Saint youth would arise at 5:30 A.M. five days a week to attend religious study classes. In the early 1970s, the home study seminary program was introduced so that Latter-day Saint students throughout the world could receive religious instruction. During President Smith's administration, seminary and institute enrollment grew dramatically.

In President Smith's last public address, given at the April 1972 general conference, he said: "There is no cure for the ills of the world except the gospel of the Lord Jesus Christ. Our hope for peace, for temporal and spiritual prosperity, and for an eventual inheritance in the kingdom of God is found only in and through the restored gospel. There is no work that any of us can engage in that is as important as preaching the gospel and building up the Church and kingdom of God on earth."[2]

After serving as Church President for two and one-half years, Joseph Fielding Smith passed quietly away in the home of his daughter. He had reached the age of 95 and had served the Lord valiantly throughout his life.

President Harold B. Lee

On the day after President Joseph Fielding Smith died, the family of President Harold B. Lee, the senior member of the Quorum of the Twelve, gathered for a home evening. One family member asked what they could do that would help President Lee the most. "Be true to the faith; just live the gospel as I have taught you," he answered. That message applies to all Church members. In his first press conference as Church President, Harold B. Lee declared: "Keep the commandments of God. Therein will be the salvation of individuals and nations during these troublesome times."[3]

When Harold B. Lee became Church President on 7 July 1972, he was 73 years old, the youngest Apostle to become President since Heber J. Grant. He had played a major role in Church administration since 1935, when he was called to direct the Church welfare program (see page 109). He had also played a major role in the review of the Church's programs and curriculum materials that led to the simplification and correlation of Church programs. He was a man of deep spirituality who was quick to respond to the impressions he received from heaven.

President Lee and his Counselors presided over the second area conference, held in Mexico City. Church members assembled at this conference were the first Latter-day Saints to sustain the new First Presidency. President Lee explained that the meetings were held in Mexico City to "give recognition and to commend the wonderful labors of the many who . . . have been instrumental in bringing about the tremendous growth of the Church."

When the Saints in Mexico and Central America learned that an area conference would be held in Mexico City, many began making plans to attend. One sister went door-to-door asking for laundry. For five months she saved the pesos earned from scrubbing her neighbors' clothes and was able to travel to the conference and attend all the sessions. Many Saints willingly fasted during the days of the conference because they did not have money to buy food after working and saving to attend the meetings. Those who made sacrifices were rewarded with great spiritual strength. One member declared that the conference was "the most beautiful experience of my life!" Another told a reporter, "It will take many years for us to forget the love that we have felt here these days."[4]

During his administration, President Lee visited the Holy Land, the first Church President in this dispensation to do so. He also announced that smaller temples would now be constructed and would eventually dot the world.

On the day after Christmas in 1973, after having served as Church President for only 18 months, President Lee died. A spiritual giant had returned to his eternal home.

President Spencer W. Kimball

A man who knew much about pain and suffering, Spencer W. Kimball, the senior member of the Twelve, was sustained as President of the Church after President Lee died. Most of his vocal cords had been removed because of cancer, and he spoke in a quiet, husky voice that Latter-day Saints came to love. Known for his humility, his commitment, his ability to work, and his personal slogan, "Do It," President Kimball thrust in his sickle with all his might.

⅊ Spencer W. Kimball's first address as President was to the Church's regional representatives, and it was memorable for everyone who attended. A participant in the meeting recalled that only moments after the talk began, "we became alert to an astonishing spiritual presence, and we realized that we were listening to something unusual, powerful, different. . . . It was as if he were drawing back the curtains which covered the purpose of the Almighty and inviting us to view with him the destiny of the gospel and the vision of its ministry."

President Kimball showed the leaders "how the Church was not fully living in the faithfulness that the Lord expects of His people, and that, to a certain degree, we had settled into a spirit of complacency and satisfaction with things as they were. It was at that moment that he sounded the now famous slogan, 'We must lengthen our stride.' " He admonished his audience to increase their commitment to proclaiming the gospel to the nations of the earth. He also called for a large increase in the number of missionaries who could serve in their own countries. At the conclusion of the sermon, President Ezra Taft Benson declared, "Truly, there is a prophet in Israel."[5]

⅊ Under President Kimball's dynamic leadership, many more members served full-time missions, and the Church moved forward throughout the world. In August 1977, President Kimball traveled to Warsaw, where he dedicated the land of Poland and blessed its people that the work of the Lord might go forward. Missionary training centers were established in Brazil, Chile, Mexico, New Zealand, and Japan. In June 1978 he announced a revelation from God that was to have a tremendous effect on missionary work worldwide. For many years the priesthood had been denied to persons of African descent, but now priesthood and temple blessings would be granted to all worthy male members.

This revelation had long been hoped for by faithful people throughout the world. One of the first black persons to accept the gospel in Africa was William Paul Daniels, who learned of the

125

Church as early as 1913. He traveled to Utah, where he received a special blessing from President Joseph F. Smith. President Smith promised him that if he remained faithful, he would hold the priesthood in this life or the next. Brother Daniels died in 1936, still a faithful member of the Church, and his daughter had the temple ordinances performed for her father soon after the 1978 revelation on the priesthood.[6]

Many more people in Africa developed testimonies of the truthfulness of the gospel through Church literature or through miraculous personal experiences, but they were not able to enjoy all the blessings of the gospel.

For many months before the June 1978 revelation, President Kimball discussed with his Counselors and the Twelve Apostles the denial of priesthood authority to persons of African descent. Church leaders were reluctant to open missions in areas of the world where the full blessings of the gospel could not be conferred upon worthy Church members. In an area conference in South Africa, President Kimball declared: "I prayed with much fervency. I knew that something was before us that was extremely important to many of the children of God. I knew that we could receive the revelations of the Lord only by being worthy and ready for them and ready to accept them and put them into place. Day after day I went alone and with great solemnity and seriousness in the upper rooms of the temple, and there I offered my soul and offered my efforts to go forward with the program. I wanted to do what he wanted. I talked about it to him and said, 'Lord, I want only what is right.' "[7]

In a special meeting in the temple with his Counselors and the Quorum of the Twelve Apostles, President Kimball asked that they all freely express their views about giving the priesthood to black males. Then they prayed around the altar with President Kimball as voice. Elder Bruce R. McConkie, who was there, later said, "On this occasion, because of the importuning and the faith, and because the hour and the time had arrived, the Lord in his providences poured out the Holy Ghost upon the First Presidency and the Twelve in a miraculous and marvelous manner, beyond anything that any then present had ever experienced."[8] It was made clear to the leaders of the Church that the time had come for all worthy men to receive the full blessings of the priesthood.

The First Presidency sent a letter dated 8 June 1978 to priesthood leaders, explaining that the Lord had revealed that "all worthy male members of the Church may be ordained to the priesthood without regard for race or color." On 30 September 1978, the Saints in general conference voted unanimously to support the action of their leaders. This letter is now found in the Doctrine and Covenants as Official Declaration 2.

Since the time of this announcement, thousands of persons of African descent have come into the Church. The experience of one convert in Africa illustrates how the hand of the Lord has blessed these people. A college graduate and teacher had a dream in which he saw a large building with spires or towers, into which people dressed in white were entering. Later as he was traveling, he saw a Latter-day Saint chapel and felt impressed that this church was somehow connected with his dream, so he attended a Sunday service there. After the meetings, the mission president's wife showed him a pamphlet. Opening it, the man saw a picture of the Salt Lake Temple, the building of his dream. Later he said: "Before I became aware I was weeping. . . . I can't explain the feeling. I was released of all burdens. . . . I felt that I had gone to a place where I visited often. And now I was at home."[9]

During President Kimball's administration, the First Quorum of the Seventy was reorganized, the three-hour consolidated Sunday meeting schedule was put into place, and temples were built at a rapid pace. In 1982, 22 temples throughout the world were either in the planning stages or under construction, by far the most in the Church's history to that time. Also, President Kimball established a demanding travel schedule that took him to many countries to hold area conferences. At these meetings, he ignored his own needs and scheduled every possible opportunity to meet with and strengthen and bless the local Saints.

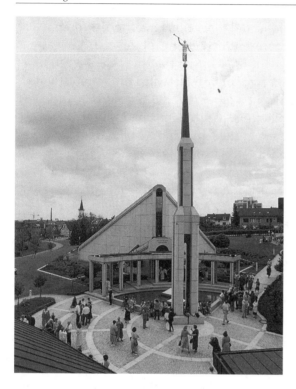

*In recent years, temples
have been built in
increasing numbers
throughout the world.
The Frankfurt Germany
Temple is one of the
many temples that now
bless the lives of Church
members.*

In many countries, Church members yearned to receive the sacred ordinances of salvation offered in temples. Among these was a Latter-day Saint from Sweden who served many missions and labored in the mission presidency. When he died, he left a substantial part of his property to the Swedish temple fund, long before the Church announced that a temple would be constructed in that country. When President Kimball announced the temple, this man's contribution had accrued interest and become a large sum. Soon after the temple's dedication, this faithful brother, who was endowed while he lived, was sealed to his parents in the very temple his money had helped to build.

A father and mother in Singapore determined to take their family to the temple to be sealed and receive their temple blessings. They sacrificed many things to raise the necessary funds and were finally able to make the trip and attend the temple. They stayed in the home of the missionary who had taught them years earlier. While visiting a grocery store, this sister became separated from her husband and the missionary. When they found her, she was holding a bottle of shampoo and weeping. She explained that one of the sacrifices she had made in order to attend the temple was to go without shampoo, which she had not used for seven years. Her sacrifices, while difficult to make, now seemed small, for she knew that her family was eternally bound together by the ordinances of the house of the Lord.

Another major development during President Kimball's administration occurred in 1979 when the Church published a new English-language edition of the King James Bible. The text was unchanged, but footnotes were added that cross-referenced the Bible with the Book of Mormon, Doctrine and Covenants, and Pearl of Great Price. A large Topical Guide and Bible Dictionary provided insights unique to modern-day scriptures. This edition had new headings for all chapters and also included excerpts from Joseph Smith's inspired revisions of the King James Bible.

In 1981 new editions of the Book of Mormon, Doctrine and Covenants, and Pearl of Great Price were also published. These included the new system of footnotes, new chapter and section headings, maps, and an index. At about this time, the Church also began to place increased emphasis on translating the latter-day scriptures into many other languages.

In his example and teachings, President Kimball inspired Church members to excellence in all their endeavors. At the celebration honoring the 100th anniversary of the founding of Brigham Young University, he said, "I am both hopeful and expectant that out of this University and the Church's Educational System there will rise brilliant stars in drama, literature, music, sculpture, painting, science, and in all the scholarly graces."[10] On other occasions, he expressed his hope that Latter-day Saint artists would tell the story of the restored gospel in a powerful and persuasive manner.

President Spencer W. Kimball with Indians in the southwestern United States.

In spite of President Kimball's busy schedule, he constantly reached out to others in love and service. He had a special feeling for the Native American people in North and South America and the people of the Polynesian islands, and he spent many hours in various efforts to help them. He had received a blessing from President George Albert Smith instructing him to watch over them, and as President of the Church, he designated members of the Quorum of the Twelve to dedicate or rededicate the lands in Central and South America for the preaching of the gospel. Since that time, tens of thousands of people throughout Central and South America have rejoiced in the blessings of the gospel.

An incident that was typical of his concern for all people occurred in a crowded airport where a young mother, stranded by bad weather, stood in line after line with her two-year-old daughter, trying to get a flight to her destination. She was two months pregnant and under doctor's orders not to carry her young child, who was exhausted and hungry. No one offered to help, although several people made critical comments about her crying child. Then, the woman later reported:

"Someone came towards us and with a kindly smile said, 'Is there something I could do to help you?' With a grateful sigh I accepted his offer. He lifted my sobbing little daughter from the cold floor and lovingly held her to him while he patted her gently on the back. He asked if she could chew a piece of gum. When she was settled down, he carried her with him and said something kindly to the others in the line ahead of me, about how I needed their help. They seemed to agree and then he went up to the ticket counter [at the front of the line] and made arrangements with the clerk for me to be put on a flight leaving shortly. He walked with us to a bench, where we chatted a moment, until he was assured that I would be fine. He went on his way. About a week later I saw a picture of Apostle Spencer W. Kimball and recognized him as the stranger in the airport."[11]

For some months before his death, President Kimball suffered with severe health problems, but he was always an example of patience, long-suffering, and diligence in the face of trial. He died on 5 November 1985, after serving as President of the Church for 12 years.

*As people throughout the world accept the restored gospel of Jesus Christ,
they are able to receive the blessings of sacred ordinances.*

132

CHAPTER ELEVEN

The Present-day Church

President Ezra Taft Benson

Ezra Taft Benson became President of the Church after the death of Spencer W. Kimball. Early in his administration, he emphasized the great importance of reading and studying the Book of Mormon. He testified that "the Book of Mormon brings men to Christ," and reaffirmed Joseph Smith's statement that this book constitutes the "keystone of our religion, and a man would get nearer to God by abiding by its precepts, than by any other book."[1]

In the April 1986 general conference, President Benson declared: "The Lord inspired His servant Lorenzo Snow to reemphasize the principle of tithing to redeem the Church from financial bondage. . . . Now, in our day, the Lord has revealed the need to reemphasize the Book of Mormon. . . . I promise you that from this moment forward, if we will daily sup from its pages and abide by its precepts, God will pour out upon each child of Zion and the Church a blessing hitherto unknown."[2] Millions around the world accepted the challenge and received the promised blessing.

Another major theme was the importance of avoiding pride. In the April 1989 general conference, he called for the members of the Church to "cleanse the inner vessel by conquering pride," which he warned was the cause of the destruction of the Nephite nation. He counseled that "the antidote for pride is humility—meekness, submissiveness."[3]

While he was serving as a member of the Quorum of the Twelve, Ezra Taft Benson had an unusual opportunity to be an example of gospel living. In 1952, with the encouragement of President David O. McKay, he accepted an appointment as the

Secretary of Agriculture under Dwight D. Eisenhower, president of the United States. This was the only time in the history of the Church that a member of the Quorum of the Twelve served in a United States president's cabinet. During his eight years of service, he gained widespread respect at home and abroad for his integrity and for his expertise in guiding and carrying out the agricultural policies of the United States government. He came into contact with leaders of nations and opened doors to representatives of the Church throughout the world.

Under President Benson's leadership, the Church made important advances worldwide. On 28 August 1987, he dedicated the Frankfurt Germany Temple in the Federal Republic of Germany, a meaningful privilege for him because he had been headquartered in Frankfurt while serving as president of the European mission from 1964 to 1965.

The Freiberg Germany Temple in the German Democratic Republic was dedicated on 29 June 1985. This dedication followed a number of miracles that occurred to make possible its construction. On his first visit to the German Democratic Republic in 1968, Elder Thomas S. Monson of the Quorum of the Twelve promised the Saints: "If you will remain true and faithful to the commandments of God, every blessing any member of the Church enjoys in any other country will be yours." In 1975, while on assignment in the same country, Elder Monson was impressed by the Spirit to dedicate that land to the Lord, saying, "Father, let this be the beginning of a new day for the members of Thy church in this land." He asked that the heartfelt desire of the Saints "to obtain temple blessings" might be fulfilled. His inspired promise and prophetic prayer of dedication were realized.[4]

On the last day of March 1989, Latter-day Saint missionaries were allowed to enter the German Democratic Republic. On 9 November 1989, the faith and prayers of many Saints were answered when the barriers between eastern and western Europe began to come down, leading to increased convert baptisms and construction of Church buildings. One convert first learned of the

Elder Russell M. Nelson with the vice president of the Russian Republic on 24 June 1991. The vice president announced that less than a month earlier, the Church had been given official recognition throughout the republic.

Church when he visited an open house in the newly completed chapel in Dresden, Germany, on 1 May 1990. Less than a week later he was baptized after he had received the missionary lessons, read the Book of Mormon twice from cover to cover, and acquired a strong testimony of the gospel's truthfulness.[5]

On 24 June 1991, at a banquet following the Mormon Tabernacle Choir's concert in Moscow, the vice president of the Russian Soviet Federal Socialist Republic announced that the Church was officially recognized in his country. This allowed the Church to establish congregations throughout this large republic. During the 1990s, a number of former Soviet republics and middle and eastern European countries were dedicated for the preaching of the gospel, including Albania, Armenia, Belarus, Bulgaria, Estonia, Hungary, Latvia, Lithuania, Romania, Russia, and Ukraine. Church facilities are being leased and built in each of these countries, and many people are gaining testimonies of the truthfulness of the gospel. At the dedication of the first Latter-day Saint meetinghouse in Poland since before World War II, Elder Russell M. Nelson of the Quorum of the Twelve prayed that the meetinghouse might serve as "a refuge of peace for troubled souls and a haven of hope for those who hunger and thirst after righteousness."[6] This blessing is being fulfilled in the lives of Saints in many countries who have found the peace and joy of the gospel.

As a result of tremendous growth in Church membership and President Benson's emphasis on missionary work, at the conclusion of his administration almost 48,000 missionaries were serving in 295 missions of the Church.

Also during his administration, the Church welfare program began offering increased humanitarian assistance to members of other faiths worldwide. This assistance is provided to relieve suffering and to foster long-term self-reliance. Large amounts of food, clothing, medical supplies, blankets, cash, and other items are distributed to the needy, and long-term projects provide health care, literacy training, and other services. This compassionate service is reaching thousands of people today in many parts of the world.

Afflicted by the infirmities of old age and the loss of his beloved wife, Flora, President Benson died on 30 May 1994 at the age of 94, having valiantly completed his mission as prophet of the Lord. He was succeeded by Howard W. Hunter, who was then serving as President of the Quorum of the Twelve.

President Howard W. Hunter

In his first news conference on 6 June 1994, President Howard W. Hunter established some of the important themes of his administration. He said: "I would invite all members of the Church to live with ever-more attention to the life and example of the Lord Jesus Christ, especially the love and hope and compassion He displayed.

"I pray that we might treat each other with more kindness, more courtesy, more humility and patience and forgiveness."

Dedication of the Orson Hyde Memorial Garden in Jerusalem on 24 October 1979. The garden, on the Mount of Olives, commemorates Elder Orson Hyde's dedication of the land of Palestine on 24 October 1841.

He also asked members of the Church to "establish the temple of the Lord as the great symbol of their membership and the supernal setting for their most sacred covenants. It would be the deepest desire of my heart to have every member of the Church temple worthy."[7] Many thousands of Church members took these messages into their lives and were blessed with a greater depth of spirituality.

President Hunter had a keenly developed mind that was of great value to the Church. In the late 1970s he received an assignment that required all his skills. He played an important role in negotiating the acquisition of land and in overseeing the construction of the Church's major building in the Holy Land—Brigham Young University's Jerusalem Center for Near Eastern Studies. This center is located on Mount Scopus, an extension of the Mount of Olives. It houses the residences and study activities of students studying in depth about this choice land, its people (Jews and Arabs alike), and the places where Jesus and his ancient prophets walked. This center has been a blessing to those who have studied within it, and its beauty has inspired many who have visited there.

President Hunter also played an important part in the development of the Polynesian Cultural Center, located adjacent to Brigham Young University—Hawaii in Laie, Hawaii. He was the founding chairman of the board for this 42-acre visitor attraction that is owned and operated by the Church. Its purpose is to preserve Polynesian culture and to provide employment for students. Built in 1963, it is a major attraction that is now visited by nearly a million people each year, who come to enjoy the music, dances, arts, and crafts of the Polynesian islands.

Before he became Church President, Elder Hunter served for eight years as president of the Genealogical Society of Utah, the forerunner of today's Family History Department. During this time, the society sponsored the first World Conference on Records in 1969, which, he said, "has created much good will for the Church and has opened doors for our work all over the world."[8] He developed a great love for all people, living and dead, and often taught that we are all part of one great family. He was known as a man who possessed Christlike love.

During his lifetime, President Hunter faced many adversities. With faith and fortitude, he dealt with serious and painful health problems, the long-term debilitating illness and death of his first wife, and other difficulties. In spite of these obstacles, he actively served the Lord, traveling much and working hard in administering the affairs of the Church. His example was consistent with his message: "If you have troubles at home with children who stray, if you suffer financial reverses and emotional strain that threaten your homes and your happiness, if you must face the loss of life or health, may peace be unto your soul. We will not be tempted beyond our ability to withstand. Our detours and disappointments are the straight and narrow path to Him."[9]

President Hunter presided in Mexico City, Mexico, on 11 December 1994 as the Church's 2,000th stake was created, an important milestone in Church history. To those assembled he said: "The Lord, through His servants, has brought this miracle to pass. This work will continue to go forward in strength and vitality. The promises made to Father Lehi and his children about their posterity have been and are continuing to be fulfilled in Mexico."[10] During the time President Hunter served as a General Authority, the Church in Latin America grew dramatically. At the time he became President of the Church, there were over 1.5 million Latter-day Saints in just the countries of Mexico, Brazil, and Chile, more Church members than lived in Utah at that time.

Although President Hunter served as President of the Church for only nine months, he had a powerful effect upon the Saints, who remember him for his compassion, long-suffering, and profound example of Christlike living.

President Gordon B. Hinckley

When Gordon B. Hinckley became President of the Church following the death of President Hunter, he was asked what would be the focus of his Presidency. He replied: "Carry on. Yes, our theme will be to carry on the great work which has been furthered by our predecessors who have served so admirably, so faithfully and so well. Building family values, yes. Fostering education, yes. Building a spirit of tolerance and forbearance among people everywhere, yes. And proclaiming the gospel of Jesus Christ."[11]

President Hinckley's extensive experience with Church leadership prepared him well for the Presidency. He was sustained to the Quorum of the Twelve Apostles in 1961. Beginning in 1981, he served as a Counselor in the First Presidency to three Church Presidents—Spencer W. Kimball, Ezra Taft Benson, and Howard W. Hunter. During some of these years, he carried extraordinarily heavy responsibilities when these Church Presidents suffered from the infirmities of age.

While young Gordon B. Hinckley was on his mission in England, he received some counsel that has served him well throughout his years of challenging responsibilities. Being somewhat discouraged, he wrote a letter to his father, saying, "I am wasting my time and your money. I don't see any point in my staying here." After some time, he received a short letter from his father that said: "Dear Gordon. I have your letter. . . . I have only one suggestion. Forget yourself and go to work. With love, Your Father."

President Hinckley said of that moment: "I pondered that, and the next morning in our scripture class we read that great statement of the Lord: 'For whosoever will save his life shall lose it; but whosoever shall lose his life for my sake and the gospel's, the same shall save it' (Mark 8:35). It touched me. That statement, that promise, in conjunction with my father's letter, prompted me to go upstairs, . . . get on my knees, and make a covenant with the Lord that I would try to forget myself and go to work. I count that as the day of decision in my life. Everything good that has happened to me since then I can trace back to the decision I made at that time."[12]

President Hinckley is well known as a person of irrepressible optimism, always filled with faith in God and in the future. " 'Things will work out' may well be President Hinckley's most repeated assurance to family, friends, and associates. 'Keep trying,' he will say. 'Be believing. Be happy. Don't get discouraged. Things will work out.' "[13]

When asked by a reporter to identify the greatest challenge facing the Church, he responded, "The most serious challenge we face and the most wonderful challenge is the challenge that comes of growth." He explained that increased growth presents the need for more buildings, including more temples: "This is the greatest era in the history of the Church for temple building. Never has the construction of temples gone forward with the momentum that is now being carried forward. We have 47 operating temples. We have 13 other temples in some course of construction reaching back to the drawing board. We will continue to build temples."[14] Increased Church growth has also made necessary the translation of the Book of Mormon into many languages.

President Hinckley has had personal experience with the dramatic growth of the Church. While attending a conference in Osaka, Japan, in 1967, he looked out at the audience, which included many young people, and said: "In you I see the future of the Church in Japan. And I see a great future. We have scarcely scratched the surface. But I feel impressed to say what I have felt for a long time, and that is that the day is not far distant when there will be stakes of Zion in this great land."[15] Within a generation, there were 100,000 Latter-day Saints in Japan, many stakes, missions, and districts, and a temple.

President Hinckley is also very interested in the growth of the Church in the Philippines, where the first stake was organized in Manila in 1973. Two decades later, at the time he became President of the Church, over 300,000 Philippine members were receiving the blessings of the gospel, including a temple in their country. President Hinckley has shown great concern for the growth of the Church in other parts of Asia as well, including Korea, China, and Southeast Asia.

The spirituality of many members in Asia is evidenced by the experience of a General Authority who was assigned to call a new stake president in a Philippines stake. After interviewing a number of priesthood brethren, he was impressed to call a man in his mid-twenties to be the stake president. He asked the young brother to go into an adjoining room and take some time to select his counselors. The brother came back in about 30 seconds. The General Authority thought he had misunderstood, but the new stake president said, "No. I knew through the Spirit of the Lord that I was going to be the stake president a month ago. I've already selected my counselors."

It is fitting that President Hinckley, who has done so much to assist in the establishment of the Church throughout the world, was able to announce during his administration: "Our statisticians tell me that if the present trend continues, then some time in February of 1996, just a few months from now, there will be more members of the Church outside the United States than in the United States. The crossover of that line is a wonderfully significant thing. It represents the fruit of a tremendous outreach."[16]

A major emphasis of President Hinckley's administration is the importance of good family life, especially in a world that often does not support family values. Under his direction, the First Presidency and Council of the Twelve issued a special proclamation to the world on the subject of the family, which states in part:

"The family is ordained of God. Marriage between man and woman is essential to His eternal plan. Children are entitled to birth within the bonds of matrimony, and to be reared by a father and a mother who honor marital vows with complete fidelity. Happiness in family life is most likely to be achieved when founded upon the teachings of the Lord Jesus Christ. . . .

"We warn that individuals who violate covenants of chastity, who abuse spouse or offspring, or who fail to fulfill family responsibilities will one day stand accountable before God. Further, we warn that the disintegration of the family will bring upon individuals, communities, and nations the calamities foretold by ancient and modern prophets."[17]

During the April 1995 general conference, President Hinckley announced that on 15 August 1995 the Church's regional representatives, who had served so well, would be released and that a new position, that of Area Authority, would be established. Area Authorities preside at stake conferences; reorganize or create stakes; provide training to stake, mission, and district presidents; and carry out other assignments given by the First Presidency and their Area Presidencies. This new position allows Church leaders to live and work closer to the people they serve and facilitates increased growth throughout the world.

One General Authority explained how each Saint can best sustain President Hinckley: "As he assumes the holy office to which he has been called—prophet, seer, revelator, Presiding High Priest and President of The Church of Jesus Christ of Latter-day Saints, . . . the best thing we can do to sustain him in his office is to 'carry on, carry on, carry on!' "[18]

These missionaries are helping to fulfill the prophecy of Joseph Smith:
"The truth of God will go forth boldly, nobly, and independent, till it has
penetrated every continent, . . . and sounded in every ear."

Conclusion

Each of us has a place in Church history. Some members are born into families who for generations have embraced the gospel and nurtured their children in the ways of the Lord. Others are hearing the gospel for the first time and entering the waters of baptism, thereby making sacred covenants to do their part in building the kingdom of God. Many members live in areas where they are just beginning their era of Church history and are creating a heritage of faith for their children. Whatever our circumstances, we are each a vital part of the cause of building Zion and preparing for the second coming of the Savior. We are "no more strangers and foreigners, but fellowcitizens with the saints, and of the household of God" (Ephesians 2:19).

Whether we are new members or old, we inherit a legacy of faith and sacrifice from those who have gone before us. We are also modern-day pioneers to our children and to those millions of our Heavenly Father's children who have yet to hear and accept the gospel of Jesus Christ. We make our contributions in different ways throughout the world by faithfully carrying out the work of the Lord.

Fathers and mothers prayerfully train their children in principles of righteousness. Home and visiting teachers care for those in need. Families bid good-bye to missionaries who have chosen to devote years of their lives to carrying the gospel message to others. Selfless priesthood and auxiliary leaders answer calls to serve. Through countless hours of quiet service given in searching out the names of ancestors and performing sacred ordinances in the temple, blessings are extended to the living and the dead.

We are each helping to fulfill the destiny of The Church of Jesus Christ of Latter-day Saints that was revealed to the Prophet Joseph Smith. In 1842 he prophesied:

"The Standard of Truth has been erected; no unhallowed hand can stop the work from progressing; persecutions may rage, mobs may combine, armies may assemble, calumny may defame, but the truth of God will go forth boldly, nobly, and independent, till it has penetrated every continent, visited every clime, swept every country, and sounded in every ear, till the purposes of God shall be accomplished, and the Great Jehovah shall say the work is done."[1]

Although the Church remained very small during the Prophet Joseph Smith's lifetime, he knew that it was the kingdom of God on earth with a destiny to fill the whole earth with the truths of the gospel of Jesus Christ. We have seen the dramatic growth of the Church in recent years. We are privileged to live at a time when we can offer our faith and sacrifices in helping to establish the kingdom of God, a kingdom that will stand forever.

Endnotes

INTRODUCTION

1. *History of the Church*, 3:30.
2. "Easter Greetings from the First Presidency," *Church News*, 15 Apr. 1995, 1.

CHAPTER TWO

1. Lucy Mack Smith, *History of Joseph Smith* (1958), 128.
2. Reuben Miller Journals, 1848–49, 21 Oct. 1848; Historical Department, Archives Division, The Church of Jesus Christ of Latter-day Saints; hereafter cited as LDS Church Archives; spelling and punctuation modernized.
3. Dean Jessee, ed., "Joseph Knight's Recollection of Early Mormon History," *BYU Studies*, Autumn 1976, 36; spelling modernized.
4. *History of the Church*, 5:124–25.
5. *The Saints' Herald*, 1 Mar. 1882, 68.
6. *History of the Church*, 1:55.
7. "History of Brigham Young," *Millennial Star*, 6 June 1863, 361.
8. Brigham Young, in *Journal of Discourses*, 3:91.
9. "History of Brigham Young," *Millennial Star*, 11 July 1863, 438.
10. "Letter from Oliver Cowdery to W. W. Phelps," *Latter-day Saints' Messenger and Advocate*, Oct. 1835, 199.
11. *History of the Church*, 1:78.
12. *History of the Church*, 1:78.
13. Lucy Mack Smith, *History of Joseph Smith*, 168.
14. Dean Jessee, ed., "Joseph Knight's Recollection of Early Mormon History," 37; spelling modernized.
15. *History of the Church*, 5:126.
16. *History of the Church*, 2:443.
17. "Conference Minutes," *Times and Seasons*, 1 May 1844, 522–23.
18. Joseph Knight Autobiographical Sketch, 1862; in LDS Church Archives.
19. Newel Knight, quoted in Larry Porter, "A Study of the Origins of The Church of Jesus Christ of Latter-day Saints in the States of New York and Pennsylvania, 1816–1831" (Ph.D. diss., Brigham Young University, 1971), 296.
20. *Broome Republican*, 5 May 1831; quoted in Larry Porter, "A Study of the Origins of The Church of Jesus Christ of Latter-day Saints," 298–99; emphasis added.
21. Lucy Mack Smith, *History of Joseph Smith*, 204.

CHAPTER THREE

1. Orson F. Whitney, "Newel K. Whitney," *Contributor,* Jan. 1885, 125.
2. Elizabeth Ann Whitney, quoted in Edward W. Tullidge, *Women of Mormondom* [1877], 42.
3. Orson F. Whitney, in Conference Report, Apr. 1912, 50.
4. Brigham Young, in *Journal of Discourses,* 11:295.
5. Orson F. Whitney, "Newel K. Whitney," 126.
6. Joseph Holbrook, quoted in James L. Bradley, *Zion's Camp 1834: Prelude to the Civil War* (1990), 33.
7. George Albert Smith, "History of George Albert Smith, 1834–1871," 17; in LDS Church Archives.
8. *History of the Church,* 2:73.
9. *History of the Church,* 2:68.
10. Joseph Young Sr., *History of the Organization of the Seventies* (1878), 14.
11. Wilford Woodruff, *Deseret News,* 22 Dec. 1869, 543.
12. "Zera Pulsipher Record Book, 1858–1878," 5; in LDS Church Archives.
13. "History of John E. Page," *Deseret News,* 16 June 1858, 69.
14. Orson F. Whitney, *Life of Heber C. Kimball,* 3rd ed. (1945), 104.
15. Orson F. Whitney, *Life of Heber C. Kimball,* 105.
16. *Eliza R. Snow: An Immortal* (1957), 54.
17. "Sketch of an Elder's Life," *Scraps of Biography* (1883), 12.
18. *History of the Church,* 2:430.
19. Daniel Tyler, "Incidents of Experience," *Scraps of Biography,* 32.
20. Eliza R. Snow, quoted in Tullidge, *Women of Mormondom,* 95.

CHAPTER FOUR

1. Emily M. Austin, *Mormonism; or, Life Among the Mormons* (1882), 63.
2. Emily M. Austin, *Mormonism,* 64.
3. Joseph Smith, *Latter Day Saints' Messenger and Advocate,* Sept. 1835, 179.
4. Larry C. Porter, "The Colesville Branch in Kaw Township, Jackson County, Missouri, 1831 to 1833," *Regional Studies in Latter-day Saint Church History: Missouri,* ed. Arnold K. Garr and Clark V. Johnson (1994), 286–87.
5. *History of the Church,* 1:199.
6. Emily M. Austin, *Mormonism,* 67.
7. *Autobiography of Parley P. Pratt,* ed. Parley P. Pratt Jr. (1938), 72.
8. *History of the Church,* 1:269.
9. *Far West Record,* ed. Donald Q. Cannon and Lyndon W. Cook (1983), 65.
10. "Newel Knight's Journal," *Scraps of Biography* (1883), 75.
11. Mary Elizabeth Rollins Lightner, *Utah Genealogical and Historical Magazine,* July 1926, 196.
12. *History of the Church,* 1:391.
13. "Philo Dibble's Narrative," *Early Scenes in Church History* (1882), 84–85.
14. *Autobiography of Parley P. Pratt,* 102.
15. "Newel Knight's Journal," *Scraps of Biography,* 85.
16. Andrew Jenson, *The Historical Record* (1888), 7:586.

17. D&C 116:1; see also D&C 107:53–57; *History of the Church,* 3:34–35.
18. Orson F. Whitney, *Life of Heber C. Kimball,* 3rd ed. (1945), 213–14.
19. Leland Homer Gentry, "A History of the Latter-day Saints in Northern Missouri from 1836 to 1839," (Ph.D. diss., Brigham Young University, 1965), 419.
20. Amanda Barnes Smith, quoted in Edward W. Tullidge, *Women of Mormondom* [1877], 124, 128.
21. Amanda Barnes Smith, quoted in Tullidge, *Women of Mormondom,* 126.
22. E. Dale LeBaron, "Benjamin Franklin Johnson: Colonizer, Public Servant and Church Leader" (master's thesis, Brigham Young University, 1966), 42–43.
23. Leland Homer Gentry, "A History of the Latter-day Saints in Northern Missouri," 518.
24. *Autobiography of Parley P. Pratt,* 211.
25. "Copy of a Letter from J. Smith Jr. to Mr. Galland," *Times and Seasons,* Feb. 1840, 52.
26. Lyman Omer Littlefield, *Reminiscences of Latter-day Saints* (1888), 72–73.
27. *History of the Church,* 3:423.
28. Matthias F. Cowley, *Wilford Woodruff* (1909), 102.

CHAPTER FIVE
1. "Journal of Louisa Barnes Pratt," *Heart Throbs of the West,* comp. Kate B. Carter, 12 vols. (1939–51), 8:229.
2. "Journal of Louisa Barnes Pratt," 8:233.
3. "Journal of Mary Ann Weston Maughan," *Our Pioneer Heritage,* comp. Kate B. Carter, 9 vols. (1958–66), 2:353–54.
4. *History of the Church,* 4:186.
5. Louisa Decker, "Reminiscences of Nauvoo," *Woman's Exponent,* Mar. 1909, 41.
6. "The Mormons and Indians," *Heart Throbs of the West,* 7:385.
7. B. H. Roberts, *A Comprehensive History of the Church,* 2:472.
8. *History of the Church,* 5:2.
9. Minutes of the Female Relief Society of Nauvoo, 28 Apr. 1842, 40.
10. Minutes of the Female Relief Society of Nauvoo, 28 Apr. 1842, 33.
11. "Journal of Louisa Barnes Pratt," 8:231.
12. *History of the Church,* 4:587, 604; 6:558.
13. *History of the Church,* 6:555.
14. Kenneth W. Godfrey, "A Time, a Season, When Murder Was in the Air," *Mormon Heritage,* July/Aug. 1994, 35–36.
15. *History of the Church,* 6:601.
16. Matthias Cowley, "Reminiscences" (1856), 3; in LDS Church Archives.
17. Thomas Ford, *A History of Illinois,* ed. Milo Milton Quaife, 2 vols. (1946), 2:217.
18. Thomas Ford, *A History of Illinois,* 2:221–23.
19. *History of the Church,* 7:230.
20. Quoted in *History of the Church,* 7:236.
21. Quoted in *History of the Church,* 7:236.
22. Quoted in *History of the Church,* 7:236.

CHAPTER 6

1. Juanita Brooks, ed., *On the Mormon Frontier: The Diary of Hosea Stout,* 2 vols. (1964) 1:114; spelling and punctuation modernized.
2. Juanita Brooks, *On the Mormon Frontier,* 1:117; spelling and punctuation modernized.
3. James B. Allen, *Trials of Discipleship: The Story of William Clayton, a Mormon* (1987), 202.
4. Russell R. Rich, *Ensign to the Nations* (1972), 92.
5. *Readings in LDS Church History: From Original Manuscripts,* ed. William E. Berrett and Alma P. Burton, 3 vols. (1965), 2:221.
6. James S. Brown, *Giant of the Lord: Life of a Pioneer* (1960), 120.
7. Caroline Augusta Perkins, quoted in "The Ship Brooklyn Saints," *Our Pioneer Heritage* (1960), 506.
8. Utah Semi-Centennial Commission, *The Book of the Pioneers* (1897), 2 vols., 2:54; in LDS Church Archives.
9. "Jean Rio Griffiths Baker Diary," 29 Sept. 1851; in LDS Church Archives.
10. "Story of Nellie Pucell Unthank," *Heart Throbs of the West,* comp. Kate B. Carter, 12 vols. (1939–51), 9:418–20.
11. William Palmer, quoted in David O. McKay, "Pioneer Women," *Relief Society Magazine,* Jan. 1948, 8.
12. "They, the Builders of the Nation," *Hymns,* no. 36.

CHAPTER 7

1. See *Journal of Discourses,* 13:85–86.
2. John R. Young, *Memoirs of John R. Young* (1920), 64.
3. Carter E. Grant, *The Kingdom of God Restored* (1955), 446.
4. Quoted in B. H. Roberts, *Life of John Taylor* (1963), 202.
5. Francis M. Gibbons, *Lorenzo Snow: Spiritual Giant, Prophet of God* (1982), 64.
6. "The Church in Spain and Gibraltar," *Friend,* May 1975, 33.
7. R. Lanier Britsch, *Unto the Islands of the Sea: A History of the Latter-day Saints in the Pacific* (1986), 21–22.
8. Charles W. Nibley, "Reminiscences of President Joseph F. Smith," *Improvement Era,* Jan. 1919, 193–94.
9. Quoted in Russell R. Rich, *Ensign to the Nations* (1972), 349.
10. *Diary of Charles Lowell Walker,* ed. A. Karl Larson and Katharine Miles Larson, 2 vols. (1980), 1:239; spelling and punctuation modernized.
11. Leonard J. Arrington, *Charles C. Rich* (1974), 264.
12. Elizabeth Wood Kane, *Twelve Mormon Homes Visited in Succession on a Journey through Utah to Arizona* (1974), 65–66.
13. Quoted in Gordon B. Hinckley, *Truth Restored* (1979), 127–28.
14. Brigham Young, in *Journal of Discourses,* 18:233.

CHAPTER 8

1. Kahlile Mehr, "Enduring Believers: Czechoslovakia and the LDS Church, 1884–1990," *Journal of Mormon History* (Fall 1992), 112–13.

2. R. Lanier Britsch, *Unto the Islands of the Sea: A History of the Latter-day Saints in the Pacific* (1986), 352–54.

3. Lee G. Cantwell, "The Separating Sickness," *This People* (Summer 1995), 58.

4. B. H. Roberts, *A Comprehensive History of the Church*, 5:592.

5. B. H. Roberts, *A Comprehensive History of the Church*, 5:593.

6. B. H. Roberts, *A Comprehensive History of the Church*, 5:590–91.

7. *Melvin J. Ballard: Crusader for Righteousness* (1966), 16–17.

8. James R. Clark, comp., *Messages of the First Presidency of The Church of Jesus Christ of Latter-day Saints*, 6 vols. (1965–75), 3:256–57.

9. James B. Allen, Jessie L. Embry, Kahlile B. Mehr, *Hearts Turned to the Fathers: A History of the Genealogical Society of Utah, 1894–1994* (1995), 39–41.

10. B. H. Roberts, *A Comprehensive History of the Church*, 6:236.

11. "Wilford Woodruff Journals" (1833–98), 6 Apr. 1893; in LDS Church Archives; spelling and punctuation modernized.

12. Richard Neitzel Holzapfel, *Every Stone a Sermon* (1992), 71, 75, 80.

13. See Matthias F. Cowley, *Wilford Woodruff* (1909), 602.

14. "The Redemption of Zion," *Millennial Star*, 29 Nov. 1900, 754.

15. "Biographical Sketches: Jennie Brimhall and Inez Knight," *Young Women's Journal*, June 1898, 245.

CHAPTER 9

1. Quoted in Serge F. Ballif, in Conference Report, Oct. 1920, 90.

2. James R. Clark, comp., *Messages of the First Presidency of The Church of Jesus Christ of Latter-day Saints*, 6 vols. (1965–75), 4:222.

3. "Editorial," *Improvement Era*, Nov. 1936, 692.

4. First Presidency, in Conference Report, Oct. 1936, 3.

5. J. Reuben Clark Jr., special meeting of stake presidents, 2 Oct. 1936.

6. For further information, see Glen L. Rudd, *Pure Religion: The Story of Church Welfare Since 1930* (1995).

7. Vincenzo di Francesca, "I Will Not Burn the Book!" *Ensign*, Jan. 1988, 18.

8. George Albert Smith, in Conference Report, Apr. 1948, 162.

9. George Albert Smith, *Sharing the Gospel with Others*, sel. Preston Nibley, (1948), 110–12.

10. George Albert Smith, in Conference Report, Oct. 1947, 5–6.

11. See Glen L. Rudd, *Pure Religion*, 248.

12. Ezra Taft Benson, in Conference Report, Apr. 1947, 154.

13. Quoted in Gerry Avant, "War Divides, but the Gospel Unites," *Church News*, 19 Aug. 1995, 5.

14. For further information, see Glen L. Rudd, *Pure Religion*, 254–61.

15. George Albert Smith, in Conference Report, Apr. 1949, 10.

16. Quoted in Llewelyn R. McKay, *Home Memories of President David O. McKay* (1956), 5–6.

17. George Durrant, "No. 1 Christian," *Improvement Era*, Nov. 1968, 82–84.

CHAPTER 10

1. Joseph Fielding Smith, in Conference Report, Apr. 1930, 91.

2. Joseph Fielding Smith, in Conference Report, Apr. 1972, 13; or *Ensign,* July 1972, 27.

3. Francis M. Gibbons, *Harold B. Lee* (1993), 459.

4. Jay M. Todd, "The Remarkable Mexico City Area Conference," *Ensign,* Nov. 1972, 89, 93, 95.

5. W. Grant Bangerter, in Conference Report, Oct. 1977, 38–39; or *Ensign,* Nov. 1977, 26–27.

6. E. Dale LeBaron, "Black Africa," *Mormon Heritage,* Mar./Apr. 1994, 20.

7. *The Teachings of Spencer W. Kimball,* ed. Edward L. Kimball (1982), 451.

8. Bruce R. McConkie, "All Are Alike unto God," *Charge to Religious Educators,* 2nd ed. (1981), 153.

9. E. Dale LeBaron, "Black Africa," 24.

10. Spencer W. Kimball, "The Second Century of Brigham Young University," *Speeches of the Year, 1975* (1976), 247.

11. *Spencer W. Kimball,* ed. Edward L. Kimball, Andrew E. Kimball Jr. (1977), 334.

CHAPTER 11

1. Ezra Taft Benson, *A Witness and a Warning* (1988), 3, 21; see also *History of the Church,* 4:461.

2. Ezra Taft Benson, in Conference Report, Apr. 1986, 100; or *Ensign,* May 1986, 78.

3. Ezra Taft Benson, in Conference Report, Apr. 1989, 6–7; or *Ensign,* May 1989, 6–7.

4. Thomas S. Monson, in Conference Report, Apr. 1989, 66; or *Ensign,* May 1989, 51; see also Conference Report, Oct. 1985, 44; or *Ensign,* Nov. 1985, 34.

5. Garold and Norma Davis, "The Wall Comes Down," *Ensign,* June 1991, 33.

6. *Church News,* 29 June 1991, 12.

7. Howard W. Hunter, *Church News,* 11 June 1994, 14.

8. Eleanor Knowles, *Howard W. Hunter* (1994), 193.

9. Howard W. Hunter, in Conference Report, Oct. 1987, 71; or *Ensign,* Nov. 1987, 60.

10. *Church News,* 17 Dec. 1994, 3.

11. *Church News,* 18 Mar. 1995, 10.

12. *Gordon B. Hinckley: Man of Integrity, 15th President of the Church,* videocassette (1994).

13. Jeffrey R. Holland, "President Gordon B. Hinckley," *Ensign,* June 1995, 5.

14. *Church News,* 18 Mar. 1995, 10.

15. Gordon B. Hinckley, "Addresses," AV 1801; in LDS Church Archives.

16. Gordon B. Hinckley, in Conference Report, Oct. 1995, 92–93; or *Ensign,* Nov. 1995, 70.

17. First Presidency and Council of the Twelve Apostles, "The Family: A Proclamation to the World," *Ensign,* Nov. 1995, 102.

18. Jeffrey R. Holland, "President Gordon B. Hinckley," 13.

CONCLUSION

1. *History of the Church,* 4:540.